PERFORMANCE CONSTELLATIONS

THEATER: THEORY/TEXT/PERFORMANCE

Series Editors: David Krasner, Rebecca Schneider, and Harvey Young

Founding Editor: Enoch Brater

Recent Titles:

Performance Constellations

NETWORKS OF PROTEST AND

ACTIVISM IN LATIN AMERICA

Marcela A. Fuentes

UNIVERSITY OF MICHIGAN PRESS

Ann Arbor

Published in the United States of America by
the University of Michigan Press
Manufactured in the United States of America
Printed on acid-free paper

First published October 2019

A CIP catalog record for this book is available from the British Library.

ISBN 978-0-472-07422-8 (hardcover : alk. paper)
ISBN 978-0-472-05422-0 (paper : alk. paper)
ISBN 978-0-472-12583-8 (ebook)

Cover photo: Sol Vazquez

Cover description: A large crowd of activists demonstrate in February 2018 in front
of the Argentine National Congress in Buenos Aires. Some raise green bandanas
that represent the struggle for reproductive rights; others point cell phone cameras
to capture the demonstration.

Performance and theatre make manifest something both more than and less than "the body." And yet the acts made visible in theatre and performance are acts we attribute over and over again to bodies, often immaterial and phantasmatic ones . . . we tend to read gestures as expressions of "authentic" selves, performances as identities. In the days ahead it will be increasingly difficult to insist on the distinction between acts of creation and identities. We are more and more only what we make, what we do. And those who are unable to make or do will have a harder time dramatizing their value.
    —Peggy Phelan, *Mourning Sex*

Is performance always only about embodiment? Or does it call into question the very contours of the body, challenging traditional notions of embodiment? Since ancient times, performance has manipulated, extended, and played with embodiment—this intense augmentation did not begin with Laurie Anderson.
    —Diana Taylor, *The Archive and the Repertoire*

In Argentina, where the multitude and its power begins, the power of the State (the power of terror) and the chaos of the market end: "Fear is over."
    —Giuseppe Cocco, *Diálogo sobre la globalización, la multitud y la experiencia argentina*

#VivasNosQueremos #WeWantOurselvesAlive
    —Ni Una Menos

Contents

Digital materials related to this title can be found on the Fulcrum platform via the following citable URL https://doi.org/10.3998/mpub.8172441

Acknowledgments

I have many people to thank for their love and support in the multinational journey that led to this book.

My mentor and friend, Diana Taylor, turned my curiosity about performance art into a fascinating exploration of the world of/as performance. Her brilliance, humor, and political commitment, together with her invitation to approach academic writing as a form of theater, imbued the early stages of this project and became the blueprint for later developments. *Gracias*, Diana, for the worlds you made possible, individually and through Hemi, and for telling me that "nobody said it was going to be easy." José Esteban Muñoz embraced my interest in the event and challenged me to think deeply about the concrete and utopian workings of performance. Thank you for "showing up" unexpectedly at that party in Buenos Aires, and for teaching me what you meant by queer worldmaking on the spot. Jill Lane and André Lepecki were also deluxe mentors in the years of my doctoral work at New York University, and they continue to inspire my work. Peggy Phelan, Richard Schechner, Barbara Kirshenblatt-Gimblett, and Barbara Browning were awesome teachers and mentors who helped lay out the foundation of my work in performance studies. They brilliantly modeled how to weave performance theory and practice, poetically and compellingly, in academia and the world beyond.

Françoise Lionnet and Shu-mei Shih have been invaluable intellectual guides and brilliant interlocutors who gave me the opportunity to explore performance through a transnational lens during my postdoctoral research in the "Cultures in Transnational Perspective" program at UCLA. I also thank my "mellow felons" Sze Wei Ang, Maya Boutaghou, Travis Workman, Sonali Pahwa, Sarah Valentine, Greg Cohen, Jeannine Murray-Román, and Joseph Bauerkemper for your engagement with my work and your fellowship. You embody the true meaning of collaboration and generous critique.

From my years at UCLA, I also thank the Department of Theater, the Department of Spanish and Portuguese, and the Department of Gender Studies for hosting my courses during my postdoctoral fellowship time. I thank Sue-Ellen Case and Susan Leigh Foster for their pointed feedback and for welcoming me to LA and to the West Coast version of performance studies. Chantal Rodríguez, Lindsay Brandon Hunter, Sara Wolf, Carla Melo, Ana Paula Höfling, Harmony Bench, Rosemary Candelario, Angeline Shaka, Lorena Alvarado, Allison Wyper, Mariel Carranza, Rafa Esparza, Micaela Díaz-Sánchez, and Raquel Gutiérrez made LA a home and a place I always love to return to. Thank you, and here's to more performance *encuentros*.

Lynette Hunter and the University of California Multicampus Research Group on International Performance, John Rouse, Peter Lichtenfeld, Frank B. Wilderson III, Leo Cabranes-Grant, Patrick Anderson, and Daphne Lei, thank you for welcoming me in your laboratory of ideas and for your provocative thoughts on performance across borders and cultures. I will never forget our reenactment of the Last Supper, directed by Case and Foster. What a treat!

Tara McPherson introduced me to the digital humanities and gave me the opportunity to dig deeper in my exploration of performance and digital media during the "Broadening Digital Humanities," NEH-funded summer institute at the University of Southern California. Thank you for making us play with Arduino and think about the materiality of the digital. Wendy Hui Kyong Chun, Nick Mirzoeff, A. Joan Saab, Mark Williams, Kara Keeling, Karen Tongson, Brian Goldfarb, Verónica Paredes, Kevin Hamilton, Ned O'Gorman, Debra Levine, and Jentery Sayers were smart and supportive colleagues who inspired me to think about performance and the visual. Craig Dietrich and Erik Loyer gave us Scalar to draft digital books, and I need to thank you for your "tags visualization" that inspired the idea of performance constellations.

At Northwestern, my academic home, the Dean of the School of Communication, Barbara O'Keefe, has been militant about the crucial role of the arts and performance in society, particularly in challenging times, and for her support and engagement of transnational dialogues and exchanges, I am deeply thankful. In my home department, I am immensely grateful for the collegiality, support, and mentorship that brilliant scholars and cultural workers such as D. Soyini Madison and E. Patrick Johnson have offered to me without hesitation since day one. My *pana* and mentor extraordinaire, Ramón Rivera-Servera, has played a huge role in making this journey more joyful and scalable. It has been amazing to work by your side and be able to bring so much of our shared love for Latin/o/a American performance to our community at NU. I am also incredibly lucky to be down the hall from my sibling Joshua Chambers-Letson and to share the excitement of discussing ideas in class visits and beyond. Thank you,

Ramón and Josh, for reading portions of my work, suggesting titles, and sharing martinis in cold Chicago days. Mary Zimmerman, Carol Simpson Stern, and Paul Edwards have been models of tireless dedication to the art of pedagogy, and I thank you for creating the vibrant and engaged artistic and scholarly platform that is Performance Studies at Northwestern. Shayna Silverstein has been a generous and warm interlocutor, and I am looking forward to more conversations about the ethics of social media research and also bike-friendly Chicago parks.

Jennifer C. Nash, Alejandra Uslenghi, Pablo Bowczkowski, Claudio Benzecry, Liz Son, Dasia Possner, Sandra Marquez, Nitasha Sharma, Miriam Petty, AJ Christian, Laura León Llerena, Nathalie Bouzaglo, Jorge Coronado, César Pinto, Mary Weismantel, Kyle Henry, Anna Parkinson, Emily Maguire, James Hodge, and Danny Snelson have been great department neighbors and intellectual partners in crime. Special thanks to Josh Honn who discussed with me the "dark" side of the internet and pushed me to think about corporate performativity. Susan Manning, Tracy Davis, and Mary M. Poole are always amazing to run into in talks or hallways, and I am honored to be their colleague. I have been also super fortunate to count on the supportive presence and expertise of Dina Marie Walters in both of her roles as departmental coordinator and Neo-Futurist performance artist.

My undergraduate and graduate students at Northwestern have also been a crucial part of my thinking as this project was taking shape. I thank them for raising critical questions in seminar discussions and through performances. I have learned a lot in seminars I led, such as Performance and Activism in Digital Culture, Transnational Flows of Performance, and Performance and Digital Media, when we honored the true mission of the university, assessing the concrete effects of performance and digital tools in people's lives. I have been fortunate to have excellent "scholartists" as research assistants: I thank Roy Gómez-Cruz, Rae Langes, Misty DeBerry, Scott Leydon, Patricia Nguyen, Benjamin Zender, and Danielle Ross for their vital help in the development of my work and for being true collaborators.

Generous funding for this project has been provided by Fondo Nacional de las Artes in Argentina, the Andrew W. Mellon Foundation, the Tinker Foundation, and the School of Communication and the Alice Kaplan Institute for the Humanities at Northwestern.

The Hemispheric Institute of Performance and Politics has also been a crucial material and intellectual supporter of my research and performance practice. Through Hemi I met incredible artists, scholars, and activists of the Americas with whom I shared the complexities, frictions, and pleasures of doing transnational work in situ. Heartfelt thanks to Jesusa Rodríguez,

Liliana Felipe, Astrid Hadad, Guillermo Gómez-Peña, Roberto Sifuentes, Peter Kulchyski, Praba Pilar, Doris Difarnecio, María José Contreras Lorenzini, Jorge Louraço Figueira, Roewan Crowe, Jarvis Robin Brownlie, T. L. Cowan, Jasmine Rault, Vivian Martínez Tabares, Antonio Prieto Stambaugh, Jorge Cerezo, Javier Serna, Doris Sommer, Silvia Spitta, Agnes Lugo-Ortiz, Diane Miliotes, Milla Riggio, Victor Vich, Fernando J. Rosenberg, Claudia Briones, Paolo Vignolo, Lilian Manzor, Luis Peirano, Leda Martins, Gina Athena Ulysse, Macarena Gómez-Barris, Lawrence La Fountain-Stokes, Carmen Oquendo Villar, Raquel Chapa, micha cárdenas, Annabelle Contreras Castro, and Hilan Bensusan, and so many others. Marcial Godoy-Anativia, Marlène Ramírez-Cancio, Ayanna Lee, Lisandra Ramos, and Niki Kekos have been indefatigable ambassadors and promoters of hemispheric cultural work and amazing "hemisexuals" that encouraged us to never forget to put pleasure and fun in the equation.

Ricardo Domínguez, Marcelo Wakstein, Sergio Gilabert, Karina Granieri, Alicia Herrero, Federico Zukerfeld, Loreto Garín, Mirta Antonelli, Sandra Mutal, Julia Risler, Patricia Avila, Hisham El-Naggar, and Diego Zenobi sat with me to talk and discuss issues like hacktivism, financial capitalism, art-activism, performativity and public capital, and socially engaged art in times of economic crisis. Even though this book took a somewhat different direction than the one that informed my dissertation, our dialogues pervade many of the ideas I share here, and I thank you for your important work.

Team *Performance Constellations* merits a special mention: Maite Málaga Iguiñiz, compas Angeles Donoso Macaya and César Barros, Iván Smirnow, Juan Santarcángelo, José Isla Hidalgo, Stella Vera Kuguel, Judy Ornelas Sisneros, Michaela Walsh, Julio Pantoja, Brenda Werth, and Paola Hernández provided generous feedback, and conceptual and research support. Thank you for reading my chapters, taking walks with me (my favorite form of critical thinking), or helping me find the photographers whose work captivated me for years. Elizabeth Heard deserves an effusive and loud, campy Thank You! because of her crucial support in the last stages of this process when the successful completion of the manuscript seemed unattainable. David Wise, Tere Carbajal, Shannon VanAntwerp, and Meagan helped me stay healthy and were also key companions in this.

LeAnn Fields has been a steady supporter of this project from the day we met to discuss its preliminary contours. I am forever grateful for her editorial expertise and guidance. I cannot think of a better editor than her for this book. I am also grateful to the anonymous readers who took my work seriously, read closely what was on the page, and brought to the fore latent ideas, pushing me to develop this project to its full potential.

My friends in Argentina, Miranda Nardelli, Valeria Cini, Vanina Estévez, Claudio Ceriani, Tano Magenta, Verónica Ezcurra, Susana Torres Molina, Silvia Pascual, Ana Rojas, and Mariana Tirantte, thank you for your love, support, and your continuous presence throughout these years. Diana Raznovich was at the beginning of it all, and I will always be grateful for her generosity and her genius. Ivana Vollaro has been a joyful and witty presence throughout, a crucial node that connected me to the ever-expanding circles of artists and activists that propelled this project.

Susana Tambutti, Yamila Volnovich, and Sandra Torlucci are former mentors and now colleagues whom I treasure each time I return to Argentina. There is something of *artes combinadas*, of what you taught me, that vibrates in these pages. Ana Alvarado gave me the opportunity to teach a seminar on performance and technology in Buenos Aires, which became a lab that jump-started my tactical media pedagogy in the North. I am grateful for that opportunity and for having been able to continue my explorations in conversation with Silvia Maldini as well.

My friends from many places that I met in the United States: Shoshana Polanco, Susana Cook, Consuelo Arias, Karen Jaime, Jude Alfaro, Masi Asare, Shanna Lorenz, Beliza Torres Narváez, Pablo Assumpção Costa, Eleonora Fabião, Brigitte Sion, Sebastián Calderón Bentín, Jaime Conde Salazar, Jo Novelli, Shayoni Mitra, Michelle Minnick, Carolinne Messihi, Anurima Banerji, Saviana Stanescu, Rodrigo Tisi, Dorita Hannah, Nikki Cesare-Schotzko, Karmenlara Ely, Olga Sasplugas, Farai Bere, Lori Cole, Sandra Ruiz, Maja Horn, Yari Taína, Sean Cook, Carla Corona, Fernando Calzadilla, Leticia Robles Moreno, and Jess Appelbaum. Some of you started grad school with me in September 2001 and made those days more bearable and actually unforgettable in their own right. You need to know I call ourselves "the Event generation."

A special mention and declaration of admiration and love to my Ni Una Menos sisters, María Pía López, Ximena Espeche, Vanina Escales, María Florencia Alcaraz, Agustina Paz Frontera, Verónica Gago, Virginia Giannoni, Cecilia Palmeiro, Marta Dillon, Mariana Carbajal, Ximena Talento, Florencia Minici, Jazmín Risé, and Luci Cavallero. Thank you for your tireless, individual, and collective work, and for welcoming me as a fellow activist, "performance doctor," and transnational comrade. I truly believe this book could not have been completed until you said #NosMueveElDeseo #VivasNosQueremos.

My mother, who grew up in the countryside in Argentina with little access to education, encouraged me to learn English and *computación*, as it was called in the 80s when I was trying to figure out how to make a living. Even though she still does not quite get what I do (we have to keep working on the "performance studies for parents" script), her wisdom and deep love have been instrumental. I also thank my late father, passionate musician and writer with whom I enjoyed discussing politics and playing Ping-Pong, for supporting my work and for his ongoing presence in my life. My sister Liliana needs to be thanked particularly as she has been at the helm of the Buenos Aires familial ecosystem for almost two decades now. I do not take your labor for granted, sis. My nephews and nieces inspire me each day, and I love to witness the worlds they, and their children, create every day. I hope that at least someone from "the gang" takes an interest in perusing what I've been up to all these years. Otherwise, I promise I will perform soon. Speaking of performance, my cousin, Margarita Molfino, has been the closest in the familial constellation to share a passion for performance art, feminism, and activism. I see her already waving at me to welcome my next project, and I hope someday we get to share the stage.

Those who write know that companion species are vital to the task: I do not think it would be an exaggeration to say that Malabar and Romeo kept me sane throughout the ups and downs of facing blank pages and enduring revision battles. They made me laugh, kept me company at the desk, stayed up late, and were patient when I was away on research trips or two hours late with their dinner. I owe you two special treats and a prompt return to our days of home soccer.

Finally, eternal gratitude to Flavia Sparacino and Ciccio Jolly Di Fava, loving supporters and fans of my performance constellations. I have been tremendously fortunate to count on their cheerful presence, and in Flavia's case, her expert contributions to my meditations on networks and better futures. Thank you for helping me navigate this process, providing charts, mind maps, and generous feedback that supported and helped me flesh out my ideas. And thank you for your imaginary protest signs demanding this book. I did not quit; here it is.

Now that everyone has been thanked (I hope), I want to dedicate this book to my sister, Susana Beatriz Fuentes, whose love is infinite and timeless. You are the first star I look for when I need critical guidance. This book is for you.

Chapters 1 and 3 are derived, in part, from an article published as "Performance Constellations: Memory and Event in Digitally Enabled Protest," *Text and Performance Quarterly* 35.1 (2015): 24–42. Portions of chapter 2 appeared as "'Investments towards Returns': Protest and Performance in the Era of Financial Crises," *Journal of Latin American Cultural Studies* 21.3 (2012): 449–468.

Introduction: Updating Protest and Activism

Hemispheric Performance Constellations

As someone who grew up during a military dictatorship, I strongly believe that massive gatherings to celebrate hard-won victories or to repudiate abusive policies are crucial democratic tools. When I was a child in Buenos Aires, attending military parades on national holidays was a family tradition. With the return of democracy, popular demonstrations offered a contrasting image of collective power. Even though social protests can be mobilized both for progressive and for reactionary aims, scholars claim that in Latin America protests offer participants an opportunity to develop political capacities that may play a transformative role beyond the mechanisms of representative, delegative politics.[1]

My drama teacher, Ita Scaramuzza, took me to my first rally in 1983. It was a rally to celebrate Argentina's return to democracy. I clearly remember getting off the subway and joining the crowd in Plaza de Mayo, across from the government palace in the city of Buenos Aires. As soon as we arrived we were greeted by one person after another. It was like joining a party. Everyone was there. For theater artists this first rally under democracy was particularly significant. They had suffered the effects of state terror closely when generals persecuted, killed, or forced radical intellectuals and activists into exile, and also intervened in drama schools, banned plays from study, and deterred students from congregating in hallways or walking barefoot.[2] After years of censorship and intense social control, that afternoon in 1983 we celebrated the freedom to assemble in public space in numbers. As feminist activist Virginia Gianonni told me in 2016 when I asked her about the use of performance as an activist tool, taking over public space collectively is one of the most radical forms of political performance. Back in 1983, in the wake of the military dictatorship, relying only on our bodies, we created a massive spectacle, a performance of radical collectivity that stood in stark contrast with the spectacles of military power that the generals had made us watch during their rule.[3] Come to think of it, demonstrations have been a central part of my political and artistic education as sites of disruptive and transformative openings.[4]

Back in the eighties, activists organized rallies through phone calls, flyers, billboards, and, of course, word of mouth. Three decades later, we not only receive news of an upcoming demonstration over email or social media, but also participate in and create the march online, galvanizing collective responses to developing events. Digital networks work as vehicles of communication toward a future street mobilization, and they also function as sites of activation in the present tense. Although *watch, comment, join, share* do not necessarily mean deep engagement—and may even entrap networked publics in a circle of hyperreactivity[5]—digital networks and interactive new media have contributed new tools to activists and supporters. These tools help organizers and social movements expand their base and spheres of action. The question then seems to be *how* to use them, and how to combine them with older activist repertoires in order to transform dissident moments into power-building movements.

Performance Constellations: Networks of Protest and Activism in Latin America focuses on the entanglement between street protests and digital networking as cocreators of insurgent collective actions.[6] Here I analyze how activists, artists, and protesters in Latin America interweave on- and offline modalities of cooperative action in order to challenge the status quo and effect social change. Rather than focusing exclusively on online activism, that is, on the internet as a separate activist platform, *Performance Constellations* looks at how on- and offline activist acts propel, shape, and sustain collective action across spatial and temporal gaps. I argue that these assemblages between physical and digital sites, body-based and digitally mediated action, and synchronous and asynchronous cooperation redefine traditional repertoires of protest and activism in ways that are key to responding to contemporary systems of exploitation and subjection.

Latin America, a region with a strong history of popular mobilization and uses of theater and performance as tools of resistance in contexts of political, economic, and social turmoil, has a lot to teach us about performative protests that, thanks to digital networks, generate connected activisms beyond borders. Social movements such as the Mexican Zapatistas that mobilized global support in the midnineties, the "movement of movements" that emerged in the post-2001 economic crisis in Argentina, the 2011 Chilean student movement, the 2014 activist mobilization in response to the disappearance of the Ayotzinapa students in Mexico, and the reproductive rights movement in Argentina, have effectively used symbolic performance across physical and digital platforms to respond to violent systems of capitalist accumulation.

Challenging critics who dismiss digital activism as "slacktivism"

("Online petitions won't do it") and street protests as futile ("Who's listening?"), I offer the concept of performance constellations as a theoretical lens to define tactics of disruption and worldmaking enabled by activist articulations of body-based protest performances and digital networking. Performance constellations are multiplatform patterns of collective action that articulate asynchronous and multisited performances.[7] As multiplatform protest performances, performance constellations respond to the challenges brought about by changing neoliberal regimes that have prompted activists to recalibrate their tactics, targets, and goals. If in advanced capitalism digital networks intensify the flow of capital and information across distances, performance constellations enable activists and protesters to scale bodily, expressive actions beyond physical space and thus link local and global struggles. In this study, performance, usually conceived as an unmediated, body-to-body system of communication between actors and spectators (or between somebody doing something and someone witnessing the doing), is also activated online or, better, across on- and offline sites of protest and mobilization. The result is constellative, connective dramaturgies that bring together fragmented, dispersed modes of participation through affective circulation.[8]

Building on the work of performance and dance scholars such as Baz Kershaw and Susan Leigh Foster who analyze the theatrical and choreographic dimensions of protests as crucial components in the radicality of contentious acts, performance constellations illuminate the specific tactics that emerge from the co-action of bodily and digitally networked protests. Through performance constellations we can discern the ways in which spatiality, temporality, embodiment, and participation, all central aspects of the doings of performance, are tactically redefined in contemporary entangled activisms that expand previous notions of social mobilization and political efficacy.[9]

Consider this: steered by the US-based collective the Electronic Disturbance Theater, in 1998 activists from all over the world "gathered" at the website of the Mexican government to stage a "virtual sit-in" to repudiate the violent repression of the Zapatista rebellion against transnational trade.[10] Or this: after a massive capital flight during the 2001 economic crisis, demonstrators in Argentina converged in pots-and-pans protests that they replicated online to denounce transnational financial speculation. Or this: in 2011, Chilean students went viral with a multicity zombie flash mob depicting the dramatic impact of education privatization on students' lives and reclaimed education as a public good. Or this: claiming "We are all Ayotzinapa," Mexican activists and international allies sustained a prolonged call for justice on- and offline on behalf of the forty-three students who in 2014 were disappeared by force.

As these examples show, through symbolic performance (a simulated sit-in, a makeshift orchestra of kitchen utensils, an impromptu choreography of undead bodies, and a collective body born from the disappeared) activists create images and affective modes of relation that seek to "win hearts and minds" and thus build counterhegemonic power. As re-elaborations of the tradition of civil disobedience, virtual sit-ins offer international publics a site-specific, networked tactic to repudiate neocolonialism in the very digital avenues that facilitate it; pots-and-pans protests transform the image of food scarcity (empty cooking items) into the source of an indignant cacophony that brings together those affected by market-oriented policies; zombies serve as embodiments of predatory, parasitic capitalism that crawl online to put an end to Pinochet-era policies; and slogans such as "We are all Ayotzinapa" transform ephemeral means such as hashtags into the pulse of a developing revolt against state and corporate alliances. In all these examples, performance as stylized, live, and contextual action spans across on- and offline networks, sparking and sustaining collective political interventions toward social justice. Performance functions in these examples as a way of "acting out" social conflicts to reveal, make sense of, problematize, and interpellate local systems of power. Performance also serves as a method to "act upon," that is, to intervene in media communication channels and consensus-making discourses that favor nomadic and abstract power conglomerates.

In the era of hypermediality, when we are constantly compelled by social media platforms to disclose "what's happening," performance "becomes itself" through its reverberation across connected platforms, materializing composite, sociotechnic (human-machine) modalities of liveness.[11] As a seemingly unmediated encounter that carries the promise of transformation of both performers and spectators, performance is now furthered and enhanced by interactive networks of communication. New technologies and activist tactics update and reinvigorate performance's commitment to the present and to utopian horizons, transforming the status quo by behaving otherwise. *Watch, comment, join, share, attend, document, replicate, recycle, connect*: performance constellations of mediated interactivity add a new spin to the politics of performance as both ephemeral *and* citational, body-based reproduction.[12]

Why does this matter? What do we gain by centering performance and digital networking as crucial components of contemporary activisms? It is crucial to recognize that performance is not merely a tool to attract attention and mobilize affective responses within the society of the spectacle; performance also sets in motion prefigurative steps toward social and political transformation in a moment of concentrated power and severely compromised democracies.[13] This is why we need to understand how activists and artists configure the ground from which to effect social transformation: the sites, pace, affects, and forms of collectivity that can foster not only *ideas* of change but also move people to *make change happen*.[14]

Take the aforementioned Ayotzinapa case. Ever since news broke in September 2014 about the forced disappearance of forty-three students enrolled in a rural teachers' school located 250 miles from Iguala, in Guerrero, Mexico, protesters took to the streets and activated social media to repudiate the Mexican government's framing of the incident as "just another episode of narco violence." One of the statements most disseminated online, "Quisieron enterrarnos, pero no sabían que éramos semillas" (They tried to bury us, but they didn't know we were seeds), exemplifies how activists used tweets, memes, and hashtags to call empowered collectivities into being. During a time when government authorities resorted to the figure of the disappeared to foreclose the Ayotzinapa case and while mass graves were discovered daily, Mexican protesters insistently circulated the phrase "They tried to bury us" as a performative motto that helped them materialize and feed the insurgent momentum. Mobilizing on- and offline as in the 2012 #YoSoy132 movement (#IAm132) activists and protesters denounced the government's demobilization strategies and transformed fear and alienation into collective determination to work for change.[15]

The social mobilization triggered by the students' disappearance evoked the Neo-Zapatista rebellion, launched in 1994 against the implementation of the North American Free Trade Agreement (NAFTA) with the cry of "Enough is enough" (Ya basta!). In 2014, twenty years later, the seed imagery used by the activists mobilized by the Ayotzinapa case captured the Mexican people's rising resolve to end the normalization of violence that the country has been undergoing since 2006, when the War on Drugs began. Reposting "They tried to bury us, but they didn't know we were seeds" over and over on social media, protesters materialized the *we* announced in the sentence. Their pulsating, digitally embodied collective complemented, extended, and expanded the *we* manifested in street gatherings and marches. The rebellious seed metaphor persisted vibrantly, announcing and symbolically bringing forth fertile revolutionary grounds.

Even though we usually do not understand online posting as a performance because this activity consists mainly of text and images and it lacks a definite temporal and spatial frame, scholars such as Zizi Papacharissi,

Wendy Hui Kyong Chun, Lisa Kember, Joanna Zylinska, and others have compellingly shown that social media platforms and new media culture are sites of self-presentation, *aliveness*, and affective transmission and attunement.[16] Online campaigns and discussions are not *performances* per se but can be approached as such in order to understand social media use as a mode of expressive and transformative (performative) behavior.

"They tried to bury us, but they didn't know we were seeds": in a few words, this slogan captures the core of this book's mission and arc. Here I provide a constellative map of multiplatform protest performances that foster collective tactics against systems predicated on individuation, disposability, and erasure. I argue that, beyond their association with an ephemeral here and now, performance and networked communication media are crucial resources that animate social change as episodic, cumulative, and translocal. By tracing how on- and offline mobilization entwine, propelling local and transnational mobilizations, *Performance Constellations* aims to offer critical lenses to analyze and assess expressive, performative modalities of collective action deployed to confront transnational hegemonic powers. Similar to the Ayotzinapa activists' image of arborescence that springs from nurtured seeds, performance constellations as a critical lens traces how activists and artists coordinate actions on- and offline to generate collective, durational events. As a figure of dispersed collectivity, the concept of performance constellations draws attention to ways that in networked cultures, performance, usually conceived as a face-to-face system of communication, shifts to become a mode of concerted action that integrates participants' actions across temporalities and localities. Performance constellations illuminate the role of performance as a means of producing collectivity from temporal and spatial fragmentation, similar to the way that constellations give shape to clusters of stars that exist in different times and in distant proximity.

This is what is at play in *Thriller por la educación (Thriller for Education)*, the 2011 flash mob that students in Chile performed as part of their mobilization for public, free, and high-quality education. Within efforts to reframe education as a matter of social rather than personal investment, students synchronized a zombie dance symbolizing irreparable decay to show the state's divestment in education and the generational cost of accumulated student debt. Before, during, and after this multicity event, students occupied virtual space with pictures and video clips of a determined collective that repudiated the continuity of Pinochet-era neoliberal policies in democratic Chile.[17] In a way that, following sociologist Veronica Gago, we could describe as part of "baroque neoliberalism," that is, as ways of doing, being, and thinking that mirror neoliberalism's calculations and affects, students employed self-fashioning platforms such as social media to reveal the effects of a system that had addressed them as entrepreneurs of their future.[18] The intertwinement of online and offline activity in performance constellations critically expanded the effect of the *Thriller* flash mob, allowing students to capitalize on the afterlife of the event by engaging those not present in the street protest. The online reverberation of the flash mob enabled students to contest debt accumulation by accumulating dissident moves across physical and digital platforms.

This networked dissemination of street protests is an integral part of current efforts to sustain civic participation beyond physical assembly. I claim this centrality in tandem with theorists of technopolitics such as Javier Toret and Rossana Reguillo. Compelling acts of dissent such as the pots-and-pans demonstrations carried out in Argentina during the financial crisis of 2001 and the *Thriller for Education* flash mob I just described exemplify how online mobilization not only expands street mobilization but configures it. This perspective that foregrounds the synergy between street and online mobilization is set in opposition to claims by Paolo Gerbaudo and others who define social media's role in contemporary protest movements as a mere catalyzer of face-to-face assemblies.[19] While I concur with Gerbaudo's expansion of Susan Leigh Foster's concept of choreography to characterize the tactical use of bodies in contemporary protests, I question his argument that online mobilization is a mere aid to street assembly.[20] Putting on- and offline mobilization in synergetic relation, I show how the embodied radicality of contemporary protests is facilitated, enhanced, and sustained by networked communication tools. The tight relationship between two seemingly disparate media—the body and digital networks—enables activists and artists to configure sophisticated forms of embodied collectivity such as virtual sit-ins or swarms and feminist "green tides," as we will see in the conclusion. Through these assemblages, activists confront neoliberal mechanisms of individualization, subjectification, and transnational transfers. My examples demonstrate this synergetic relation as it is expressed in response to Western Hemispheric histories of neoliberal governance and governmentality, to which I turn next.

NEOLIBERALISM: AN "INVISIBLE HAND" SHAPING THE SOUL

"Economics are the method. The object is to change the soul": Margaret Thatcher's infamous statement in 1981 reflects the scope of neoliberal capitalism as a political economic doctrine and a mode of subjective modulation, that is, as both a top-down system of governance and of self-directed governmentality. This sentence by Thatcher—a political figure who, together with Ronald Reagan and Augusto Pinochet, became one of the global icons of neoliberalism—introduces us into the twentieth-century upgrade of eighteenth-century liberalism.[21]

As a political economic philosophy, eighteenth-century liberalism embraced human dignity and individual freedom as supreme values allegedly warranted by the market rather than the state.[22] Within liberal thought, the state and any form of collective endeavor were seen as a threat to individual freedom. This political philosophy focused on the idea that humans are best served if they are free to exercise their entrepreneurial tendencies and skills without state interference and within an environment that protects property rights, free trade, and the free market.[23]

Adam Smith's metaphor of "the invisible hand of the market," developed in *The Wealth of Nations*, illustrates the central role played by the market and self-interest in classical liberalism.[24] Smith uses the invisible hand to signify an organic process; his theory establishes that the balance between personal interest and social gain is attainable through market transactions without state intervention. These ideas signal the transition from sovereign to liberal forms of governance and the attendant association between economic and political freedom.

Although conservatives generally praise neoliberalism as a political economy that minimizes state intervention in the interest of entrepreneurial production and commerce, this is far from reality. The "invisible hand" is actually attached to very concrete bodies and powers. Rather than reducing their intervention on trade matters, twentieth-century neoliberal states become crucial players in processes of wealth accumulation propelled by policies of market and financial deregulation, privatization of state-owned companies, labor flexibilization, and reductions in social programs.

In the United States, neoliberalism was implemented as a reaction to the welfare state policies of the 1930–1960 period.[25] Following the 1960s challenges to the US economy due to global competition and falling profit rates, the neoliberalization of the US economy sought to restore power to the elites. Lisa Duggan defines US neoliberalism as "pro-business activism."[26] According to Duggan, this approach relied on a political and cultural project that created tolerance of widening inequality and support for upward redistribution. Ronald Reagan's "trickle-down economics" argument to advocate for income and capital gains tax cuts mirrors Smith's theory of the invisible hand as a mechanism of economic equilibrium.

However, these theories have actually promoted the interests of elites, positioning those economically disadvantaged as individually responsible for their shortcomings.

As we will see, neoliberal regimes favor national and transnational capital, working in tandem with financial networks, international lending institutions, and multinational corporations to ensure the legal and repressive resources needed to safeguard specific trade interests. Neoliberal states enforce property rights, create new market conditions by privatizing sectors such as education, health care, and defense, and deregulate commercial activity, thereby allowing cheap imports to dominate national and local markets.[27] This is how neoliberalism, originally conceived as a theory of economics, became a *process* that shapes transnational trade as well as modes of governance, that is, matters of the state.

A theory of neoliberal political economy thus turned into a process of neoliberalization that consolidated in the twentieth century's neoliberal state. Under the guise of the "small government" interdict, the neoliberal state ostensibly rolls back social provisions while it maximizes its role as a repressive force to deter, contain, or crush dissent from all who resist social segregation, exploitation, and displacement.

Because in Chile, Argentina, and Mexico—the main sites this book engages with— neoliberalism has been implemented by both authoritarian and democratic regimes, these countries stand out as compelling sites for the study of neoliberal forms and mutations and of the ensuing popular responses to them.[28] In Chile, the origins of neoliberalism date back to Augusto Pinochet's dictatorship and his team of US-trained economists. As part of a Cold War effort, in the 1950s the so-called "Chicago Boys" received their formative instruction in free market capitalism from economists Milton Friedman and Arnold Harberger at the University of Chicago. Before staple neoliberal figures such as Margaret Thatcher and Ronald Reagan entered the neoliberal state scene, the Chicago Boys helped Augusto Pinochet develop a program that gave Chile sustained economic stability while broadening social inequality.

Pinochet rose to power in 1973 with a violent US-backed coup against the socialist government of Salvador Allende, a Marxist physician and politician who had been elected in 1970.[29] Hence, the first implementation of neoliberalism as a state political economy rather than as a political economic philosophy took place under military rule. It inaugurated a series of neoliberal coups such as those of Argentina and Bolivia that employed what Naomi Klein calls "the shock doctrine" to activate the economy while deactivating popular opposition through repression and trauma.[30]

To characterize the foundation of neoliberalism in Argentina, Gago uses the image of the holding cells located in the headquarters of the national bank alongside a clandestine trading desk. This shows the deep entanglement between the military state and transnational financial networks during the 1976–1983 period, which militants define as a "civic and military" dictatorship.[31] In Argentina, military power not only was used to persecute and eliminate political dissidents, from union leaders to social workers and teachers, but also helped elites benefit from legal instruments such as the Financial Institutions Law of 1977 to increase their profit. As we will see in chapter 2, in Argentina the process of liberalization of the economy initiated in the 1970s through authoritarian rule was intensified in the 1990s under democratic rule through the transfer of sovereign decision-making to institutions such as the International Monetary Fund via massive debt.

Even though in Mexico the military did not seize power, as in Chile and Argentina, the hegemony of the Partido Revolucionario Institucional (Institutional Revolutionary Party) that ruled from 1929 to 2000 turned the idea of Mexican democracy into a simulation, as Subcommander Marcos declared during the Zapatistas' insurgency in the midnineties.[32] Nevertheless, until the late eighties Mexico implemented statist and nationalistic policies. This was reversed when Carlos Salinas de Gortari, who became president in 1988, implemented a series of market-led reforms (including NAFTA) promising that this would give Mexico First World status. Salinas privatized 252 state-run companies and reduced state subsidies. This economic model had a disastrous effect on peasant economies and ways of life and would also deepen social inequalities, causing the displacement of peasants and putting marginalized populations such as poor women in conditions of extreme vulnerability, as evidenced in the current femicide crisis.[33]

"Enough is enough. . . . We are the product of five hundred years of struggle," stated the Neo-Zapatistas when in 1994 they revolted against NAFTA as a new instantiation of colonial violence. Chilean students enacted a similar gesture in 2011 when they danced as zombies to dramatize the effects of the Pinochet-era education system on their lives, thus connecting contemporary predatory lending to authoritarian violence. Similarly, in Argentina, Ni Una Menos's 2015 statement, "Contra nuestros cuerpos nunca más" (Against our bodies never again), placed the current war on women as part of a lineage of state-sponsored violence against those who resist exploitation.[34]

The 1994 Zapatista insurgence, the social protests in post-2001 Argentina, the 2011 zombie flash mobs and participatory protest performances during the "Chilean Winter," the 2014 transnational mobilization after

Ayotzinapa, and the Argentine feminist movement against gender violence that emerged in 2015 all articulated body-based and digitally networked performance to produce and sustain the public appearance of those affected by neoliberal capitalism across different contexts and histories. These movements exemplify a politics of radical embodied presence that is crafted by bridging online and offline modes of collective action. As capitalism becomes increasingly speculative and dehumanizing, multi-platform expressive acts that mobilize the appearance of politically excluded—and often physically disappeared—bodies become crucial materializations of collective power as well as tactics that put into question neoliberal subjectivation.[35]

On- and offline performances configure spaces of appearance where, as Hannah Arendt states in *The Human Condition*, "I appear to others as others appear to me, where men [*sic*] exist not merely like other living or inanimate things, but to make their appearance explicitly."[36] By opening spaces of appearance that connect histories and geographies of oppression, the transmedia embodied actions mapped out here disrupt "the increased tolerance of widening inequality and support for upward redistribution."[37] Thus, revolutionary horizons open via performances that bridge private and public space, speech and embodiment, the present and history.[38] This is how we move from street protest performances to performance constellations that, as Judith Butler claims, enable those whose existence has been rendered precarious by "racism and forms of calculated abandonment" to manifest "the right to be recognized."[39] Performance as normative and subversive expressive behavior is a crucial tool in formations of collective disobedience within neoliberal conditions.

PERFORMANCE:
AN ART OF ACTIONS IN THE ERA OF NEOLIBERAL MUTATIONS

Performance is an expansive concept. In the field of performance studies, we approach performance as an object of study, an analytic lens, and a method of inquiry and intervention. "Performance" might refer to artistic, cultural, or political events such as a theater play, a music concert, or a protest (events that are set apart from everyday life); or it might be used as a way of looking at social behavior as a sort of "theater of life" where social actors engage with an explicit or implicit audience, adhering to or subverting social markers such as gender identity, national allegiance, familial roles, and race.[40] As a method of inquiry and intervention, performance produces and communicates embodied and situated knowledge about the world. And it also *makes* worlds, transforming social relations, attitudes, values, and modes of self-understanding. In this sense, performance not only reproduces what exists but it actualizes possibilities for worldmaking through consciousness-raising.

For example, feminist movements such as Ni Una Menos (NUM) rely on on- and offline performance to disentangle social roles from gendered bodies and to build emancipatory social relations. In their 2016 campaign "Con amor o sin amor, las tareas domésticas son trabajo" (With or without love, housework is work) NUM reframed maternal care as unpaid labor. Approaching women's duties as normalized exploitative performances rather than instinctual maternal care, NUM detached women's work from its usual association with gender-specific love. Once performance is used as an analytic to disentangle socially constructed identities from gendered bodies, other performances become possible as a method of transformation of oppressive systems. In their holiday campaign #EstamosParaNosotras (#WeWorkForOurselves) NUM proposed to recircuit feminized care as communitarian work, asking women to place a black ribbon on their doors or on their body to identify themselves as potential allies of women suffering domestic violence. Participants then shared selfies and other images with the group to populate their Facebook page. This campaign, launched during Christmastime and right at the start of the vacation season, which signify prime time for women's tireless labor, enacted a critique of social orders that create a false natural link between bodies and social roles. It also put in action a world in which women support and protect each other rather than being enclosed in the domestic sphere, which most times turns out to be lethal, as the current crisis of gender-based violence that gave origin to NUM demonstrates. As this example makes clear, performance as structured behavior not only maintains social orders; performance also creates conditions for change, making it possible for people to understand the constructed, contingent, and unstable status of embodied meanings and hierarchies.

Beyond performance studies' theoretical and methodological approaches to performance, visual arts scholars define it as an ephemeral, time-based, interdisciplinary art practice that emerged at the turn of the twentieth century as part of European avant-garde movements such as futurism, Dadaism, and surrealism, and was revised in the post–World War II period by collectives such as the Gutai Group and the Viennese Actionists.[41] As an art practice made "out of actions," performance is based on an existential focus on the "act" as a response to historical events such as the Holocaust and the atomic bomb, events said to exemplify the magnitude of the human capacity for destruction.[42] Thus framed, performance or *live art* enacts a dialectic between creative and destructive acts that, as critic Paul Schimmel claims, is informed by a concern for beginnings and ends.[43] As an art genre, performance is focused on process rather than product, and on endurance and duration rather than static materiality and objecthood.

As stylized acts that may involve acting upon oppressive conditions rather than merely representing them (as we saw in the example of the Ni Una Menos collective), the performance protests that are part of *Performance Constellations* can be placed within the trajectory that Uruguayan artist and theorist Luis Camnitzer identifies as "Latin American conceptualism."[44] According to Camnitzer, Latin American conceptualism actively integrated politics in artistic events and objects. Working in turbulent contexts, Latin American artists strove to make their practice socially relevant and approached art as a form of agitation. Latin American artists judged the avant-garde's aesthetic autonomy as reactionary and elitist, and in many cases followed closely the revolutionary processes initiated by political militants in the 1960s subsequent to the Cuban revolution.[45]

In Spanish-speaking countries, performance art (that is, performance as an artistic practice) has been termed *arte de acción* (action art), a concept that highlights the ephemeral, time-based, aspects of this art form.[46] Derived from the Latin *agere*, "action" means "setting something in motion," as opposed to "making" or creating a static object or product.[47] In a move that resonates with the concept of performance constellations, Spanish critic Martí Peran offers the term *arte del acontecimiento* (event art) and states that, while action art highlights processes of dematerialization within the visual arts, "event art" characterizes works in which media and agents engage with various communities. Peran defines "the event" as an ephemeral appropriation of public space that seeks to produce a territory of encounter extending "beyond the functional to the expressive."[48] We can think of the Electronic Disturbance Theater's digital performances (virtual sit-ins and HTML conceptualism pieces) as examples of event art that turn the internet into an expressive medium, bringing together protest, media, and art repertoires to create an event that disrupts protocols of networked communication.

Emphasizing the aesthetic, ethical, and tactical significance of performance as a dematerialized art of actions/events that produces a critical encounter between performers and spectators, scholars such as Peggy Phelan claim that liveness, that is, the time-based experience of the work as it is being produced, is the defining feature of performance. In Phelan's work, performance is defined as a cultural form that "becomes itself through disappearance," that is, an ephemeral presence that turns into absence.[49] In this theorization, technologies of capture—a still photograph, a video recording—deliver the *memory* of the performance, but they fundamentally differ from the performance itself.[50] Photography and film, or video recording, are not only ontologically different from live performance but also *secondary* to the ephemeral act, a means that has no impact in the constitution of the actual performance as a vital happening.

Think of Marina Abramović's iconic durational performance that was part of her 2010 retrospective *The Artist Is Present* at MoMA. Online pictures show the artist as she engaged spectators one by one over a period of seven hundred hours, simply stationed at a table during seven hours, six days a week, from March 14 to May 31. Those who were there experienced the performance, took an active part in its unfolding. Those who watched pictures or video recordings online accessed the documentation of the performance. Their viewing and their mediated presence had no way of altering the event. The categorical split between performance as a live act and "old" media communication technology (characterized as a memory or document of the performance that is parasitic to it) prevented scholars from assessing the generative aspects of technological mediation. Even though some performance works such as Ana Mendieta's *Silueta* series or Chris Burden's *Shoot* were conceived *for* the camera, liveness (understood as *unmediated presence*) was and still remains one of the defining features of performance.

In dialogue with new media studies, theater and performance studies scholars are changing how they theorize the relationship between performance and media communication technologies. The main shift entails transforming the categorical differentiation between the live act and its mediation into a phenomenological imbrication, understanding liveness as an effect of processes of mediation. Theorists such as Steve Dixon and Philip Auslander claim that in digital culture liveness and presence are the result of *demands* made by mediated events (think of Facebook's newsfeed) on participants, demands that force the audience to consider them as forms of "nowness."[51] As a mode of heightened engagement, presence is not about the "fleshiness" of a body performing in front of a live audience, but rather about the symbolic framing of a collective incident as a real-time happening that compels spectators to participate.

As anyone who has recently participated in a flash mob, a street protest, or a Twitter campaign can attest, in what social media theorist danah boyd calls the "always-on" lifestyle of wireless communication, liveness and embodiment are redefined as the effect of our interlinked online and offline interactions.[52] Participants lining up to be part of Abramović's immersive performance during the First Performance Biennial in Buenos Aires in 2015, heavily posted pictures on Facebook before reaching the moment when the crew took their smartphones so that they would focus on the actual activities scripted by the artist. At the same biennial, participants in Martín Sastre's performance *Eva: Volveré y seré performers* (Eva: I will return and I will be performers) who were invited to access the famous balcony from which Evita addressed the Argentine people enjoyed taking selfies and sharing their experience online.[53] Instead of engaging with the imaginary masses that glorified Evita in Plaza de Mayo, a group of participants favored their social media feeds as the real stage where to address *their* cheering audience. The mediated experience took precedence over the "unmediated" (albeit imaginary) encounter. Social media as storytelling platforms par excellence absorbed the auratic energy of the direct relation with a historic space offered by Sastre. "Live to tell" won over "embody to feel."

Social media dissemination is today an integral aspect of our encounter with live events. Social media posts, including still photos, videos, GIFs, and memes, which are almost in sync with actual happenings, are not merely documentary, parasitic records of live events. They expand contemporary performance's drive toward audience participation, enabling transversal dialogue among actual and potential audience members. In examples of participatory performance such as *Eva: I Will Return* digital communication networks play a generative rather than secondary role, impacting the experience and reception of live events. Through social media real-time effects, characterized by what Esther Weltevrede, Anne Helmond, and Carolin Gerlitz term the "relevance and freshness" of social media users' posts, the experience of performance as a shared happening transcends the copresence between performers and spectators that we associate with the stage concert or the performance art showing.[54]

Besides projecting offline experiences online, networked performances are characterized by a feedback loop between on- and offline networks of communication. In performative protests such as the flash mob *Thriller for Education* the experience of the street protest performance was expanded and sustained by online participation. Even though flash mobs are characterized by participants' synchronous occupation, or swarming, of physical space, in *Thriller for Education* digital communication platforms shaped the experience of the protest. The video capture of the protest and its circulation on social media transformed the in situ, time-specific performance into a distributed, extended event. Users' ongoing social media updates enabled participants to turn a memory of a performance that had a beginning and an end into the experience of an unfolding event, reaffirmed by new stagings of the flash mob in various Chilean cities.

Examples such as *Thriller for Education* turn performance as a body-based action in shared time-space into a multiplatform, distributed event. The works I analyze in this book prove that performance is not something that belongs exclusively in the offline world and that is later translated to online platforms. Rather, performance is a symbolic mode of action that connects physical and digital environments and situated/physical and virtual spaces, thus configuring transmedia actions. In networked culture, the existentialist assertion of the "here and now" that sets live performance apart from documentary reproduction is recast through the assemblage of cross-platform, multisited gestures that collectively make up a performance event.

Performance thus turns into performance constellations, and the clear-cut differentiation between the bodily, unmediated, framed event and its networked dissemination, replication, and amplification is upset. When Diana Taylor defined performance as body-to-body "acts of transfer" of memory, her approach challenged Peggy Phelan's concept of performance as that which disappears.[55] My work builds on Taylor's theorization to define contemporary activist performances as a mode of collective, mediated presence, achieved through the assemblage of dispersed actions within a common frame or narrative.

The protest performances I analyze *entangle* on- and offline networked behavior; they thereby configure multiplatform tactics that address and grapple with contemporary systems of exploitation and control that are nomadic and multilocated. Simultaneously, performance constellations that link dislocated spatialities and temporalities allow us to *disentangle* the eventness of these performances (that is, their compelling appeal and disruptive force) from its rootedness in physical and temporal copresence. In this way, we can use performance as an analytic lens to address uses of networked technology that catalyze coordinated action offline. Yet we can—and should—also frame these issues as part of the field of digital activism.

DIGITAL ACTIVISM: HOW TO DO THINGS WITH NETWORKS

To track and theorize the networked tactics used by activists in Latin America that prompt and sustain collective action, *Performance Constellations* engages with the fields of tactical media, technopolitics, and social media activism. These represent different approaches to digital activism as a mode of counterhegemonic action. In our journey into exploring the gradual entanglement between body-based performance and digital networking in Latin American social movements that mobilize against neoliberal globalization, we start with the notion of tactical media, and the practices and principles of so-called electronic civil disobedience exemplified by EDT's virtual sit-ins. The Critical Art Ensemble (CAE), a US-based group founded in the 1990s, defined tactical media as a movement not committed to a particular form or medium but rather one that employs the media that are most effective to intervene in a particular context.[56] This form of media activism grew out of the belief that street protests had lost their efficacy for fighting contemporary power configurations that are deterritorialized and networked. Media theorist Rita Raley observes that such tactical media practices create relational processes between artists and activists and their audience rather than processes of one-way communication. Openness and contingency are key elements of what Raley terms "tactical media performances," which disrupt protocols of interaction and use in order to foster unforeseen possibilities within networked systems of communication.[57]

In the South American context, pieces like *NN-Red* by Ciro Múseres and *Buscar justicia* (Justice search) by the collective Sienvolando exemplify a tactical use of the internet as a site and generator of collective engagement. Before the emergence of Facebook filters to show solidarity and allegiance, Múseres invited MSN users to change their profiles and display the image and name of a disappeared person from the last military dictatorship in Argentina. Conceived as a collective action, the piece was launched on March 24, 2006, on the thirtieth anniversary of the military coup. Sienvolando carried a similar tactical media action to demand justice in the case of Maximiliano Kosteki and Darío Santillán, members of the Unemployed Workers Movement who were killed by police in June 2002 when they blocked a bridge in the province of Buenos Aires. As part of a multisited campaign connecting on- and offline interventions, six years after Maxi's and Darío's massacre, in 2008 Sienvolando created a net art action, mainly an interactive web page that simulated the Google search interface. Sienvolando's artists replaced Google's logo with drawn images of the murdered activists' faces. Google's brand image was also modified, featuring the name of the site of conflict: the city of Avellaneda.[58]

In *Buscar justicia* the two clickable frames that are part of Google's search function were used to denounce and highlight the government's attitude toward the case: "Google search" was transformed into "Cajoneo del gobierno" (Government's inaction). This clickable frame led to a list of more than a thousand cases of police brutality without resolution. The

Figure 1: *Buscar justicia* (Justice search), net art piece by Sienvolando, Argentina, June 2008.

other option, "I'm feeling lucky," celebrated the users' active involvement in the case with the phrase "Voy a buscar justicia" (I am going to search for justice). Clicking on this option, users accessed information on the state of the legal process. The adapted Google page was also reproduced offline, as a mural on city walls, at Sienvolando's art space, and on T-shirts, suggesting that we should be as active in our demands for justice as we are in our daily Google searches.

Although 1990s open publishing and media activist projects such as Indymedia were not conceived as "tactical media" per se, they played a crucial role in the development of the alter-globalization movement, and in enabling practices of citizen journalism that transformed international audiences into active participants in local and globalized protests. In this sense, as we will see in the context of the post-2001 financial crisis in Argentina, Indymedia and media activist platforms are the antecedent of current day social media mobilization, even though these platforms belong to the one-to-many communication era.

The emergence of ubiquitous technologies that allow users to access the internet from anywhere has destabilized notions of digital activism as exclusively situated online. The digital world, no longer a novel, separate space to which we must "log on," now pervades our lives, shaping how we navigate space and social relations. Whereas in the 1990s and early 2000s activists focused on how to turn the internet into a site of protest (either replacing or complementing street demonstrations), in the 2010s, using smartphones and social media platforms, activists connect on- and offline mobilization. This paradigmatic shift, whereby technological means are used tactically and strategically in the organization, communication, and performance of collective action, is conceptualized by social movement theorists such as Toret as "technopolitics." Toret states that technopolitics is more than cyberactivism in that it appropriates or invents digital tools to generate collective action and networked organization. Technopolitics is not clicktivism; rather, "it launches tactics and strategies of communication" reducing the participation threshold, the role of intermediaries, and the cost of organizing.[59] Moreover, technopolitics assumes a multilayer form, entangling physical urban spaces, the mass media, and social networks. The so-called cycle of 2011 insurrectionary movements such as the Arab Spring, the Spanish 15-M, and Occupy Wall Street are exemplary cases of technopolitical collective action, also theorized as decentralized or "distributed democracy."[60]

When scholars analyze movements such as the Spanish 15-M and the Arab Spring, they either emphasize or downplay the role that digital mediation played in catalyzing social mobilization. Some, like Gerbaudo, argue that social media *precipitated* street assembly, which he positions as the main site of mobilization today. Others, like Toret, use the notion of augmented reality to show the juxtaposition between physical and digital environments in contemporary movements and how, through new tools, street and online protests become transmedia, diffused events.

However, media analysts on both sides of this divide tend to leave bodies behind, stressing modes of communication, cooperation, and collective intelligence across media without regard to modes of *performance*, that is, embodied, time-based, and collective action modes that assemble asynchronous and remote modalities of collaboration. As Zizi Papacharissi shows in her study of networked affect in contemporary politics, when we access and share information about a street protest in an era of pervasive digital mediation we are not merely "reporting about" but "tuning in" to the experience of a political or media event.[61] Even though Papacharissi uses discursivity to explain social media activism and affect online, her work aligns with my more performance-oriented approach to networked activism as configuring a cross-platform, extended event that redefines notions of embodiment, copresence, and liveness.

Recent spam attacks on activist hashtags foreground digital networks as spaces of symbolic contention. In light of these and other happenings such as the use of Twitter as a tool of governance, digital activism should not be dismissed as slacktivism or lazy digital activism. As Papacharissi claims, digital networks not only are a medium of communication; they also shape the way we intervene in political processes and social conflicts, inducing or shutting off personal and collective responses. Linking performance theory, political economy, and new media analysis, *Performance Constellations: Networks of Protest and Activism in Latin America* offers a methodology to trace patterns of collective protest and activist performance that rely on the synergetic relation between on- and offline environments.

UNFOLDING PERFORMANCE CONSTELLATIONS

The performance constellations that I conceptualize in this book map out nascent forms of networked activism and protest launched by Latin American organizers and supporters in response to mutating forms of neoliberal capitalism such a transnational trade, financial speculation, predatory lending, and narco violence. These shape-shifting performance constellations demonstrate that new media communication technologies do not displace performance's fundamental reliance on body-based, collective acts but update it, enabling activists to use embodied, situated mobilization to respond to increasingly abstract *and* biopolitical exploitative conditions.

The first chapter, "Assembling Convergence Online: NAFTA, the Zapatistas, and the Electronic Disturbance Theater," opens upon the scene of the celebrated "first postmodern revolution": the 1994 Zapatista insurgency against NAFTA constituted the foundation of global activist tactics to respond to local neoliberal crises. This chapter explores how activists assessed the changing mechanisms and channels of transnational capitalist accumulation that NAFTA exemplified and devised tactics that extrapolated street convergence to the internet. In this chapter, I revisit the Electronic Disturbance Theater's 1990s tactical media experiments known as "electronic civil disobedience." I explore how EDT's virtual sit-ins and practices of HTML conceptualism redefined offline notions of embodiment, copresence, and site-specificity, turning a technological, abstract performance into an experience of collective and disruptive presence. By charting how these protest performances configured performance constellations of convergence, I demonstrate that they counteracted forces that employ digital networks as abstract, disembodied, timeless channels of capital circulation.

Whereas chapter 1 establishes that online convergence was an effective tactic to activate remote, global responses to the neoliberal colonization of Zapatista land and resources, chapter 2, "Articulating Local and Global

Resistance: Fugitive Capital and On-/Offline Protests in Argentina," analyzes how early 2000s activists integrated street protest and web-based activism as tools to address the transnational dimensions of local crises. Here I focus on the 2001 economic crisis in Argentina, a crisis that prefigures the 2008 global meltdown, as a paradigmatic example of how activists used on- and offline environments to configure what I define as "stream-out" performance constellations. I analyze practices of citizen journalism, digital storytelling, and online pots-and-pans protests to reveal how their tactics used the digital against mechanisms such as abstraction, separation, and decontextualization that benefit financial capital. I argue that the stream-out performance constellations assembled during the post-2001 crisis period created conditions of radical democracy capable of responding to transnational systems of finance and to compromised sovereign states.

Shifting gears from the web-based activisms of the midnineties and early 2000s to social media activisms, the third chapter, "Expanding Moves, Enacting Futurity: Debt Governance, Transmedia Activism, and the Chilean 'Fearless Generation,'" focuses on the 2011 student protests in Chile. Here I argue that, entangling street performance and social media mobilization, activists were able to denounce individual indebtedness as "debt governance" and disentangle it from financial subjugation. I contend that, through multiplatform protest performances such as viral flash mobs, demonstrators generated tactics of networked asynchronous collaboration through which they challenged neoliberal logics of individual progress and generated conditions for alternative civic engagement.

Chapter 4, "Contesting Disappearance after Ayotzinapa: State Terror, Hashtags, and the Pulsating Event," focuses on the hashtag protests launched after the disappearance of the forty-three Ayotzinapa students previously mentioned. Chapter 4 elucidates how hashtags linked liveness and memory to form flickering, pulsating performance configurations to resist state and corporate violence. I show how, working between the passing and yet repetitive new media processes exemplified by emergent and decaying hashtags, Mexican activists transformed short-term responses into a persistent protest movement. I argue that the instability of hashtags, their characteristic *liveness* that constitutes a digital rhythm of generation, degeneration, and regeneration, is a crucial feature for activists who seek to sustain the momentum of networked protests and build revolutionary social movements.

In the conclusion, "Together We Are Infinite: Projecting Performance Constellations," I return to Argentina, more specifically to the 2018 reproductive rights mobilization, or the "green tide," to offer a final meditation on contemporary social movements as forms of "mediated togetherness." I show how current revolutions such as the feminist movement in Argentina are propelled by both activist genealogies and social media organizing and forms of activation that are decentered and contingent. I address the challenges faced by activists and protesters in an increasingly repressive, conservative, and violent political moment, and define the book's examples as *breathing templates* to be reanimated.

As dance activist and theorist Lucia Naser stated in one of her Facebook posts in late 2016, "To tell the history of what resists is also a way of thinking how transformation happens."[62] This study, which tracks performance constellations, their tactics, their contexts, and histories as they developed over time, is an invitation to consider how performance as expressive, symbolic behavior can become (or *has* become) a transformational tactic that expands across platforms, media, temporalities, territories, and historical contexts to reclaim *liveness* for those whose lives are in question, devalued, colonized. As I hope to demonstrate in the following pages, crafting performance constellations that assemble insurgent bodies to disrupt emergent modalities of subjection that have roots in colonial and authoritarian pasts, activists and artists in Latin America have created and nurtured the seeds that prefigure long-term social justice.

As governments in Latin America return to already traveled paths (resorting, for example, to international lending institutions such as the IMF whose enforced policies have had catastrophic effects in the region), activists and artists also find themselves revisiting the activist toolbox left by their predecessors—a genealogy, a memory reservoir. In that sense, performance constellations are not only about street/online entanglements; they are also meant to account for the relationship between emergence/emergency and history. Event, unfolding, and memory. Traces of the past that help bring forth possible futures.

ONE | # Assembling Convergence Online

NAFTA, the Zapatistas, and the Electronic Disturbance Theater

"JOIN ZAPATISTAS AROUND THE WORLD." With these words, digital activists directed listserv members and email recipients to click on a link where readers accessed key information about the violent campaign that the Mexican government had launched against the Zapatista insurgency. A few clicks into the online action, readers turned into participants, reaching a web page that contained several windows linked to the websites of the Mexican administration and multinational corporations. Every three seconds the images contained in the windows reloaded. *Hello, hello, hello. Page request. Client connecting to server.* Sitting alone, in front of their computer screens, participants may have felt that their actions were accomplishing little. Unlike street protests, in this online demonstration there were no bodies, no cardboard signs in view, no sound—only flickering images of home pages reloading, one after another. When the set time frame was reached—sometimes twenty-four hours after the start of the protest—the collective action came to an end. "THANK YOU." Without knowing the exact number of protesters, or where they came from and how they looked, those who took part in this digital demonstration turned critical awareness about a case of social injustice into an active response to it.

This online protest is called a "virtual sit-in." It is a form of web-based demonstration devised in 1998 by the US collective the Electronic Disturbance Theater (EDT). The EDT's first virtual sit-ins were organized in support of the Zapatista uprising against NAFTA, the North American Free Trade Agreement between Mexico, the United States, and Canada. As the Mexican government escalated the repression of the Zapatista insurgence in Chiapas, international activist groups resorted to the internet to disseminate information about the conflict and to create networks of action-based solidarity with the rebels.

The EDT's virtual sit-ins replicate Mahatma Gandhi's nonviolent civil disobedience tactic, famously employed in the context of India's struggle for independence from Britain and during the 1960s civil rights movement in the United States. At a time when the internet was promoted as a democratic venue, by "sitting in" on targeted websites activists sought to bring attention to the violent repression of local resistance against trade and finance conglomerates.

In the same way in which physical sit-ins disrupt business as usual by blocking traffic or impending regular city operations, virtual sit-ins sought to disturb data flow, that is, information exchange between servers and internet users. To achieve this, the EDT used a hacking technique known as a distributed denial of service attack (DDoS). Such attacks on a computer network clog the transfer of information between computers by overwhelming servers with excessive connection requests.

When compared to today's hacking techniques, these mid-1990s online tactics may seem obsolete. However, the EDT's performances of what they call "electronic civil disobedience" are foundational examples of digitally networked protests that sought to contest transnational systems of exploitation. At the dawn of the opening of the internet to popular use, governments in the Americas employed networked communication to favor transnational commerce by eroding land and labor rights. By contrast, the EDT provided a galvanizing tool for protesters to denounce state-corporate alliances and help consolidate the emergent antiglobalization movement. In a new iteration of tactical deployments of performance as a tool of resistance, the EDT's events of collective presence materialized "new modes of corporeal engagement,"[1] achieved through the entanglement between online and offline modes of action. In this sense, the EDT's practices of electronic civil disobedience update performance's political commitment to embodied action in order to respond to the challenges brought about by nomadic, networked, transnational capitalism.

Facilitated by the implementation of the graphical browser that expanded the internet beyond email to the hyperlinked information space that we know as the World Wide Web, the EDT's virtual sit-ins linked conceptual art, political performance (in the tradition of civil disobedience, agit-prop theater, and *teatro campesino*), and 1990s practices and philosophies of so-called tactical media.[2] Tactical media practitioners called for an interventionist rather than informational use of media and offered the concept of electronic civil disobedience as a way of recalibrating tactics in order to respond to dispersed and expedient networks of power.[3]

Through participatory performances in support of the Zapatista struggle, the EDT animated sophisticated practices of embodiment beyond actual bodies, creating opportunities for supporters to split from the immediacy of their sensory capacities in order to disrupt the speed of informational flows.[4] In the same way in which the Zapatistas used performance and discursive practices to recast the image of the "invisible Indian" into a fully embodied political agent, thus interrupting racist colonial legacies, the EDT employed symbolic performance to mobilize international solidarity as a tangible collective presence online.

Online protests such as the EDT's virtual sit-ins constitute paradigmatic examples of ways in which performance, as a form of expressive behavior conveyed through the medium of the body, is translated or transmediated to digital space. The EDT's online protests configure forms of digital embodiment, produced as relational accomplishments between participants' actions and technological operations rather than through immersive virtual reality technologies.[5] In the context that we are exploring, that is, the Americas in the era of neoliberal global redesigns and state violence, the transformation of the body from organic medium to digitally mediated presence is a tactical move. Instead of approaching the internet as a disembodied space where digitization flattens physical properties into numbers—a phenomenon that N. Katherine Hayles describes as "when information lost its body"[6]—the EDT's acts of electronic civil disobedience reconnected digital space with bodies affected by the smooth circulation of capital enabled by informational networks.

Moreover, through this adaptation of civil disobedience from physical space to digital networks, activists rallied transnational audiences in becoming actively involved in local conflicts with transnational roots. In the EDT's virtual sit-ins, the copresence in time and space that characterizes the embodied politics of performance is creatively reconfigured by entangling digital and symbolic modes of coordinated action. The EDT's virtual sit-ins exemplify ways in which performance as a symbolic framing of networked operations generates an experience of convergence for participants who intervene remotely from dispersed localities in synchronous coordination.

Although the EDT defines virtual sit-ins as "more than email and less than code,"[7] meaning that these digital actions are less disruptive than hacking and more direct than information campaigns, virtual sit-ins today are treated as criminal activity. Views about the legitimacy and efficacy of virtual sit-ins vary widely. For example, hacktivist groups such as Anonymous claim that DDoS attacks resemble street blocking or trespassing, and are thus legitimate methods of exercising citizens' rights. State agencies such as the FBI and the Secret Service deem virtual sit-ins a cybercrime, arguing that, even if hacktivists do not aim to permanently destroy servers, their actions bring chaos to the internet, potentially attracting criminals and terrorists.[8] However, the EDT's members distance themselves from hackers, framing virtual sit-ins as "performance art." They stress that their goal is not "technological efficiency" as in hacking, but "symbolic efficacy" as in the workings of cultural performance.[9] This means that, just as critical performances do, virtual sit-ins do not aim to cause mayhem but to draw attention to conditions of exploitation and oppression.

Virtual sit-ins as performance art create agonistic scenes that challenge neoliberal arrangements, usually predicated on the violent exclusion of marginalized populations, through collective assembly.[10] While previous studies—for example, Jill Lane's foundational research—have focused on how the EDT transformed the allegedly disembodied, abstract space of the internet into a public sphere, here I frame virtual sit-ins as performance constellations of embodied remote convergence.[11] Such framing allows us to analyze the ways in which, bringing together remote participants and human and nonhuman agents, the EDT demonstrated the crucial workings of digital networks as platforms of hegemonic power and collective resistance. As performance constellations of convergence, virtual sit-ins materialized modes of digital collectivity that sought to mine the power of transnational conglomerates in the very channels that facilitate their entrenchment.

Nevertheless, as we will see in the next pages, for however sophisticated their digital protest tactics were, the EDT's virtual sit-ins were not just contributions from the West to the insurgent Zapatistas. The EDT actually drew from and expanded on the Zapatistas' use of new media as tactical tools. Digital networked communication was vital to the Zapatistas, whose uprising was hailed as the "first postmodern revolution" because of the movement's investment in autonomous, bottom-up, consensus-based structures of governance rather than on institutional takeover.[12] Inspired by Zapatismo and its on-the-ground practices of resistance and social organization, the EDT contributed a digitally mediated tactic that facilitated a performance of global solidarity. In their virtual sit-ins, the EDT employed the contingent, open, and processual mechanisms of networked media communication to create performance constellations of embodied convergence as collective disruptions of networked systems of exploitation and subjection.

ZOOMING IN ON SITES OF RESISTANCE

NAFTA, the North American Free Trade Agreement signed in 1992 by the United States, Canada, and Mexico, is a paradigmatic example of the process of neoliberal globalization. NAFTA embodies the fundamentals of neoliberalism: a deregulated economy favoring markets, states' withdrawal from social programs, downward pressure on wages and working conditions, thus benefiting corporate profit, and natural resource extraction.[13] In Mexico, particularly on Zapatista land, this system deeply affected indigenous communities and campesinos due to the inflow of cheap imports and the privatization of their land.[14] NAFTA cast Mexico as a market to place commodities and products from industrially scaled agriculture, with the GMO industry radically altering the production of crops such as maize, which has been a central, organically grown ingredient of the region's food culture since preconquest times.

Whereas NAFTA consolidated the alliance between neoliberal states and transnational institutions in order to facilitate transborder trade, an emergent social movement in the Chiapas region, Zapatismo, involved a different kind of networking, in this case between indigenous communities, a leftist guerrilla movement, and later, international activists linked by anticolonial, antineoliberal, and antiglobalization principles. Zapatismo—a leftist guerrilla movement launched by the Ejército Zapatista de Liberación Nacional (EZLN or Zapatista National Liberation Army)—was born in 1983 in the Lacandón jungle in Chiapas, a southern Mexican state bordering Guatemala.[15] On January 1, 1994 (NAFTA's start date), the Zapatistas took over six large municipalities. With the cry of *Ya basta!* (Enough is enough), a group of six hundred people occupied the city hall of San Cristóbal de las Casas, a highland urban center in Chiapas. Through a document known as the "First Declaration of the Lacandón Jungle," the Zapatistas introduced themselves to the world as "the product of five hundred years of struggle." They framed their occupation as an insurrection against the "undeclared genocidal war" carried out by the Mexican government, which the Zapatistas deemed illegitimate.[16]

This first Zapatista declaration initiated a series of public addresses or *comunicados* that reached international audiences through mass media and the internet.[17] At a local level, the Zapatista *comunicados* called for a reorganization of participatory politics and for the end of the politics of exclusion of indigenous Mexicans, intending to break the monopoly that turned Mexican democracy into a scandalous simulation. At a global level, these speeches reenergized political discourse and inspired activists that later identified as part of the alter-globalization movement that made news in Seattle in 1999, when activists held a massive protest against the World Trade Organization.

The iconic Subcomandante Insurgente Marcos was the Zapatistas' spokesman until May 2014. Marcos's title of "*sub*commander" represents the Zapatistas' ethos of *mandar obedeciendo* (to lead by obeying). This means that within the Zapatista movement leaders follow collective decisions reached by consensus in open assemblies. The principle of *mandar obedeciendo* is practiced as part of the Zapatistas' political philosophy of "good government," and set in contraposition to Western systems of governance, which the Zapatistas define as examples of "bad government." One of the Zapatistas' mottos, "A world where many worlds fit," conveys a politics of multiplicity and possibility that includes minoritarian ways of life as well as a range of tactics that, as we will see, rely heavily on symbolic practice and networked communication.

The Zapatistas and their multilayered "ways of doing" toward social justice and real democratization in Mexico offer a rich site to launch this book's exploration of performance constellations as tactics of relation, interdependence, and collectivity. First, "to lead by obeying" implies a dialectical relationship between those who govern and the governed rather than the transfer of authority that defines representative democracy. It is a paradoxical formula: common sense does not usually associate obedience with leadership. Like many Zapatista principles such as "the mask that reveals," which I analyze later, this relation, this understanding of leadership as interdependent, disrupts the notion that social orders are necessarily hierarchical and seemingly fixed and uncontestable. Second, the motto "A world where many worlds fit" replaces a temporal, developmental (typically modern) view of indigeneity as "stuck in time" for a relation of spatial copresence that valorizes the coexistence of different ways of knowing and being. Third, "A world where many worlds fit" unsettles the increasingly tolerated exclusionary logics of neoliberal development, advancing worldmaking principles of inclusion and collective responsibility toward those in the margins.

As hemispheric performance scholar Diana Taylor argues, the Zapatistas are "experts on resistance."[18] Their carefully crafted public appearances include spectacular acts such as their January 1, 1994, insurgency, and their 2001 caravan walk to Mexico City as well as more communal meetings such as the 2014 farewell to Marcos that I narrate at the end of this chapter. This exemplifies the Zapatistas' broad spectrum of tactics

that include guerrilla warfare, negotiations with the Mexican government, poetic communiqués, international meetings, and the development
of autonomous municipalities that host their own education and health
systems. The Zapatistas used both event-based appearances and more
sustained practices to turn the vulnerability imposed on indigenous and
peasant communities by oppressive systems of governance into a powerful tool to engage hegemonic power.[19]

A crucial element in the Zapatistas' tactics is their use of black, knitted
masks. The Zapatistas' iconic masks evoke a tradition of Mexican mask-
performance that spans from popular entertainment in the practice of
lucha libre to its parodic use by performers such as Superbarrio Gómez.[20]
The Zapatista mask functions instrumentally to protect the identities of
insurgents. Described by Subcomandante Marcos as "a mask that
reveals,"[21] the mask also plays an expressive function.[22] The Zapatista
mask is another example of their use of paradox: whereas in a practical
sense the mask conceals individual identity, in a symbolic sense it brings
forth the compelling appearance of a collective that has been rendered
invisible. The Zapatista mask enhances and intensifies the group's public
appearance, becoming one of the symbols of Zapatismo as "the masked
face which today has a name."[23]

Performance as a form of stylized appearance played a crucial function
in the Zapatistas' embodied expressive and instrumental tactics for engaging local and global audiences in their struggle. Through their elaborate
speeches and performances of collective presence, the Zapatistas expanded
local and global awareness of neoliberalism as a continuation of colonial
violence. Using poetic discourse and embodied tactics of political intervention, the Zapatistas disrupted the limits of what Jacques Rancière calls "the
distribution of the sensible," that is, the horizon defining what can be said,
perceived, and discussed pertaining to the lives and value of indigenous
peoples.[24] Not only did indigenous people "show up" on the local and
global political stage; they did so by employing performance as a compelling border-crossing resource to generate global cooperation through channels usually reserved for those in positions of privilege.

The Zapatistas' speeches and the compelling traces of their collective
appearances in public transcended their local contexts of intervention, traveling globally thanks to activist networks that followed closely the events
in Chiapas. Thus, the Zapatista insurgence propelled the emergence of a
global movement that sought to respond to the effects of transnational capital on local communities by building solidarity across borders. These
activist networks constituted the precondition to the EDT's configuration

of performance constellations of convergence, which drew from the Zapatistas' poetics of collective presence and contributed to the expansion of the Zapatista rebellion into a global Zapatismo.

ACTING TRANSNATIONALLY: DIGITAL ZAPATISMO

Just as neoliberalism relies on digitally networked systems to connect sites of transnational production and investment, the Zapatista insurgency of 1994 and the subsequent development of a transnational Zapatismo heavily relied on digitally networked mobilization.[25] But how was this accomplished when in Chiapas many communities do not have access to electricity, let alone computers? Several nongovernmental organizations working in the region helped transmit Zapatista messages node by node so that Zapatista news would reach crucial points. A first message sent by email to a group of supporters was distributed through multiple circuits using the then-popular bulletin boards and listservs—the precursors of today's blogs and social media. These forums enabled activists and scholars from all over the world to follow the conflict closely and create a collective response to it.

Cultural critic Fiona Jeffries describes the online and offline networking by groups coming from different backgrounds as "the opposite face of the 'information revolution' as [these groups] consciously work towards creating a new communicational commons that simultaneously links and transcends space and time."[26] Although Jeffries frames the activists' use of the internet as a tool of communication rather than as a site of protest, her concept of a "new communicational commons" that connects participants across space and time resonates with the workings of performance constellations that assemble remote localities and temporalities.

The Zapatistas' tactics to gain international support, however, not only relied on digital networks but on face-to-face gatherings. On July 28, 1996, the Zapatistas welcomed thousands of participants from Mexico and other countries to their First Intercontinental Encuentro for Humanity and Against Neo-Liberalism, also called La Intergaláctica. The meeting was held in the town of La Realidad, one of the Zapatistas' autonomous municipalities. Activists from forty-three nations defied the Mexican government's military blockade and joined the Zapatistas in their territory. The encuentro concluded with a proposal to create a nonhierarchical, distributed solidarity network based on this face-to-face meeting. The next year, the Zapatistas were invited to the second encuentro, which took place in Spain with more than three thousand participants. In this meeting, activists focused on identifying shared goals and targeted the second ministerial conference of the World Trade Organization in Geneva in May 1998 as their forthcoming site of disruption.

Building on the Zapatistas' multiple tactics and on the developing alter-globalization movement, the EDT's founder, Chicano artist and activist Ricardo Dominguez, devised activist methods that would transform the internet from a channel of communication into a site of performative dissent. The EDT launched its first performance of electronic civil disobedience in support of the Zapatista insurgency in April 1998.[27] The group developed its technique for staging virtual sit-ins from previous digital actions carried out by the Italian activists of the Anonymous Digital Coalition (ADC). Immediately after the massacre of forty-five indigenous townspeople by paramilitary forces in Acteal, Chiapas, on December 22, 1997, the ADC sent a call for an action titled *Netstrike for Zapata*. The ADC's call instructed

> all the netsurfers with the ideals of justice, freedom, solidarity and liberty within their hearts, to sit-in the day 29/01/1998 from 4:00 p.m. GMT (Greenwich Mean Time) to 5:00 p.m. GMT in the following five web sites, symbols of Mexican neoliberalism: Bolsa Mexicana de Valores, Grupo Financiero Bital, Grupo Financiero Bancomer, Banco de Mexico, Banamex.[28]

To "sit-in" on these institutions, potential participants were directed to enter in their browsers the listed web addresses and to manually hit the "return" or "enter" keys multiple times. Through the action's targets—the five financial institutions considered "symbols of Mexican neoliberalism"—the ADC drew critical connections between the conflict unfolding in Chiapas and transnational capital. In this way the activist group countered the Mexican government's claim that the Acteal massacre had been carried out by unknown agents. The ADC's action laid out the groundwork for an activist transformation of the internet from information medium to performance site. The Italian activists provided the metaphor (netstrike) and the mechanism (repeated file requests) that would transform the circulation of information into a concrete, spatialized protest.

Perfecting the ADC's technique, the EDT's members Carmin Karasic and Brett Stalbaum created the Zapatista Tactical FloodNet, a web-based program that automated protesters' page reloads. Embedded in the EDT's HTML pages, once triggered by participants, FloodNet sent repetitive file requests to the targeted servers.[29] Thus, the EDT furthered the notions of online spatiality and embodiment that would be crucial to configure performance constellations of convergence.

A few months after the *Netstrike for Zapata*, on April 10, 1998, Dominguez and the EDT organized their first virtual sit-in on the website of Mexican president Ernesto Zedillo. Eighteen thousand people from all over the world participated.[30]

Like the *Netstrike for Zapata*, the EDT's virtual sit-in was based on the client–server structure of the internet as a network of connected computers. As I mentioned earlier, the technical name of this tactic is Distributed Denial of Service (DDoS). Typically, DDoS attacks may be conducted efficiently by a single hacker. The EDT's virtual sit-ins, however, required many people to intensify its effects.

Although experts on hacktivism such as Gabriella Coleman judge this to be a sign of poor technological performance, FloodNet's inefficiency actually foregrounds the EDT's philosophy of collective action that aligns with Zapatista principles.[31] That is, the core of the EDT's actions lies not in showing technological skill (as in hacker culture) but in facilitating collective dissent through digital means that update the politics of bodily protest and liveness to the informational era. Rather than seeking to perform a skillful and defiant trespassing, the action aims to show a unified front (a swarm, actually), potentially broadening the activist base beyond the circles of global justice advocates. This is done in the action itself and in the telling of the action in reports to mainstream media.[32]

In one of the first studies on the group, performance studies scholar Jill Lane argues that the EDT's practices of civil disobedience turned the internet from an informational space into a public sphere that counteracted hegemonic uses of digital information networks. Drawing from theories of embodiment and spatiality as socially and discursively constructed (rather than as a preestablished property of organic bodies or physical spaces), Lane argued that the EDT materialized embodied resistance in cyberspace discursively, circumscribing the web as a contested terrain. Through metaphors such as "virtual sit-in," the EDT staged a collective occupation, troubling narratives that framed the Net as a neutral "information superhighway" or as an "electronic frontier," thus updating colonial worldviews.[33]

Lane's theory of virtual sit-ins as discursive performances that transform the internet into a public sphere can be further expanded by fleshing out the notion of embodiment, a crucial component in practices of symbolic, tactical performance. By framing their DDoS as a "virtual sit-in," the EDT provided participants with a mental representation of embodied action (a sit-in) that relies on what performance historian Joseph Roach calls "kinesthetic imagination," that is, a way of "thinking through movements—at once remembered and invented."[34] My suggestion for framing digital embodiment as built on kinesthetic imagination underscores the fact that embodiment or bodily experience collapses the distinction between body/mind and object/subject.[35] While we usually think of embodiment as something that has to do with real, organic bodies as bounded selves located in physical spaces, embodiment or bodily perception always already involves interactive processes, feedback and feedforward loops between production, signification, and representation.[36]

In fact, media theorist Mark Hansen defines the human as "a being distributed into nonoverlapping sensory interfaces with the world," a definition that draws attention to the blurred condition of "our selves" that extends beyond the confines of the skin.[37] Thus, as it has now become part of the everyday experiences of those with access to smart and wireless networks, technology is not an extension of bounded embodied life (a tool at hand) but an integral part of our mixed-reality condition. Without recourse to contemporary high-tech virtual reality technologies, the EDT's virtual sit-ins created an experience of embodied participation that was based on core mechanisms that are foundational to our "being in the world."[38]

Besides creating an experience of embodied participation by relying on the image of the traditional sit-in and on digitally mediated interaction, virtual sit-ins employed synchronous participation, generating a sense of spatial contiguity or copresence.[39] This aspect is crucial to my conceptualization of virtual sit-ins as performance constellations of convergence, which furthers previous understandings of the EDT's digital actions as spatial, embodied tactics of disturbance.

PERFORMING NETWORKS

To understand virtual sit-ins as performance constellations of convergence, that is, as performances that articulate collective action from disjointed participation, we need to focus on networks, particularly on their workings, and on processes that networks facilitate and intensify. Although the term usually appears in relation to computers and social media, networks inform many aspects of human life, from our brains to systems of communication such as snail mail delivery. The development of microelectronics-based, software-operated communication technologies has facilitated the extension of bodies and minds through networks of interaction that process flows or streams of information. This sociotechnical change is the outcome of the microelectronics revolution of the 1940s and 1950s that provoked a paradigm shift in the 1970s, ushering in what Manuel Castells calls the "network society."[40] Digital electronics technologies facilitated an exponential increase in the capacity of systems to process information, impacting the volume, complexity, and speed of networked transfers. The increase in systems' processing power contributed to further the capitalistic logic of accumulation, enabling the globalization of production, circulation, and market transactions and offering capitalists increasingly advantageous opportunities.

Simultaneously, networks introduce new actors and forces in the process of social organization. Because informational networks enable different communication vectors between the nodes of the network, actors performing counterpower in the network society are able to craft their own communication routes and behaviors with relative autonomy from power centers.[41]Alexander R. Galloway and Eugene Thacker define the network as "a dominant form describing the nature of control . . . as well as resistance to it."[42] A key term in Galloway and Thacker's theory of networked control and resistance is "protocol," which encapsulates the rules and standards that regulate relationships within networks, whether social, technological, or biological. For Galloway and Thacker, protocol comprises principles of relationality that are also principles of political organization.[43]

Galloway and Thacker's work aims precisely to draw attention to the imbrication of technics and politics at play within networks, usually praised as forms of nonhierarchical and nonbureaucratic organization. However, networks regulated by protocol are the embodiment of rhizomatic and distributed forms of control.[44] Even though networks are typically conceived as timeless channels of communication, they involve the coexistence of multiple political structures as well as fields of force relations that unfold over time. Networks may include several, even contrasting, topologies or relational forms constituted by nodes and connective lines that Galloway and Thacker call "edges."[45]

This view of networks as spaces of possibility, as spaces of contestation of hegemonic relational arrangements which are contingent rather than fixed or neutral, aligns with the notion of performance constellations. Performance constellations, configured by the synergy between performance (as expressive or symbolic doing) and digitally networked communication. represent a particular mode of resistance that engages with the protocols of networked capitalism. In theorizing networked performances as performance constellations I am building on the work of new media theorist Anna Munster, who through her concept of "network aesthesia" or "feeling networks" draws attention to how networks structure human experience by conjoining human and nonhuman behavior.[46] Like Galloway and Thacker's project, network aesthesia and performance constellations reframe networks as *dynamic and temporal configurations*, an approach that counters sociologist Castells's definition of informational networks as flattening time.[47] These theorizations of networks as modalities of control and resistance further previous understandings of cyberspace as a *discursive space*, incorporating attention to the temporal, affective, and relational specificities of networked infrastructures that are integral to their political function.

With these approaches to the politics of networks in mind, we can now turn to what the EDT calls HTML conceptualism, another type of networked performance devised by this group to assemble collective protest and speak truth to power. As the next example illustrates, the EDT's poetic digital disturbances function as tactical disruptions of capitalist networks, introducing density and accumulation into relational forces striving to compress, flatten, and shrink time to favor transnational exploitation.

BODY REQUESTS: 404 FILE NOT FOUND MESSAGES AS HUMAN-MACHINE PERFORMANCES

An additional example of the EDT's tactics configuring performance constellations of collective, networked action in support of the Zapatista struggle is their 404 File Not Found campaigns that entangle human and nonhuman forms of agency. Through a sort of "call and response" exchange with web servers, the EDT created what performance studies scholar Jon McKenzie calls "machinic performances." The concept of machinic performance invites a focus on the generative function of digital networks rather than on their role as mere data transmitters.[48]

Like in virtual sit-ins, in their 404 File Not Found campaigns the EDT targeted institutions allegedly linked to the displacement of Zapatista communities. In these campaigns, participants prompted servers to declare these institutions' responsibility in the violent repression of the Zapatista rebellion. More importantly, these performances sought to bring out the voices of those who had been disappeared to the other side of neoliberalism at a moment in which this political economy was praised as an ideology of freedom, social equilibrium, development, and First World status.

As mentioned before, in April 1998 the EDT organized a virtual sit-in targeting the website of President Zedillo in response to the Acteal massacre, wherein they also carried out what they call "HTML conceptualism" or 404 File Not Found performances.[49] Like virtual sit-ins, the EDT's conceptual HTML performances were executed using the group's FloodNet program. However, rather than merely launching a program that automated data requests, in the EDT's 404 File Not Found performances participants used a form published on the group's website and entered their own words to launch their data requests. For example, participants could enter inexistent web addresses such as http://www.xxx.gb.mx/human_rights, prompting the Mexican government's server to respond, "Human rights not found on http://www.xxx.gb.mx." Similarly, participants were able to add the names of the Acteal victims to their searches, generating statements such as "Veronica Vasquez Luna not found on http://www.xxx.gb.mx." In this sense, 404 File Not Found campaigns functioned as ephemeral graffiti created through the unconventional use of networked protocols in order to repudiate the Mexican government's military campaign in Chiapas.

Whereas virtual sit-ins built on the tradition of civil disobedience as a choreography of defiance of spatial protocols, HTML conceptualism disturbed networked protocol by transforming a technological mechanism (data request) into an event of collective denunciation. This is similar to today's use of hashtags such as #FueElEstado (#ItWasTheState), which was part of the protests following the disappearance of the Ayotzinapa students. Instead of simply creating a web page to memorialize the Acteal victims and expose the government's role in their demise, the EDT created an interactive performance that transformed the Mexican government's servers into coperformers within a machinic performance constellation.

The EDT's File Not Found performances are, like virtual sit-ins, networked participatory experiences that seek to recreate forms of embodied, affective engagement within activist communities dedicated to information dissemination. Like virtual sit-ins, 404 File Not Found online performances employed symbolic action as the affective connector that creates alliances between participants located in disjointed spaces toward a performance of remote collectivity.[50]

As an embodied digital action that addresses the vulnerable life conditions of indigenous and peasant communities within neoliberal globalization, the EDT's conceptual HTML piece in remembrance of the victims of the Acteal massacre resonates with the practices of human rights activists such as the Mothers of Plaza de Mayo, who demanded, and still do, the restitution of their children alive ("Aparición con vida" / We want them alive). Conducting symbolic digital searches and prompting servers to "confess" human rights violations, the EDT and those who participated in the conceptual HTML piece demanded justice for the Acteal victims, framing an issue as ongoing, despite the state's attempts to shut down the request of legal responses. The Mothers' and the EDT's tactics, as well as the use of hashtags in the search for the forty-three Ayotzinapa students discussed in chapter 4, not only keep the memory of political dissidents and victims alive; they also resist the politics of erasure that characterizes atrocious genocidal acts and state-mandated foreclosure in Latin America and beyond.

In virtual sit-ins and HTML conceptual pieces, the EDT creates digitally mediated acts of embodiment to confront protocols favoring networked capitalism. In this way the EDT crafts, without completely breaking the established protocol, a poetic disturbance by which absent bodies (the "invisible Indian" or the Acteal victims) are made virtually tangible. Participants in digitally mediated performances activate symbolic gestures that enable vulnerable bodies to have powerful effects on transnational political stages. In articulating performance constellations of convergence on the internet as a site of protest, the EDT not only provided an additional space of contention, but also materialized networked bodily density, counteracting forces that employ digital networks as abstract, timeless channels of capital circulation.

THE ENDS OF PERFORMANCE CONSTELLATIONS: EVALUATING PERFORMANCE IN NETWORKED CULTURES

Because the EDT's virtual sit-ins and 404 File Not Found human-machine interactions are tactical performances whose goal is to intervene in a conflict rather than simply express a point of view or disseminate information, it is necessary to assess these actions' contribution to social movements or processes that seek to challenge and dismantle abusive conditions. We can explore the question of the EDT's impact on real-world scenarios, the EDT's expressive and instrumental effects, by focusing on the two meaning-making systems that structure their work: tactical media and theater.

As already mentioned, concepts such as "electronic civil disobedience" emerged in the context of the tactical media movement as a method to tackle changing configurations of power enabled by digital networks. Fostering a tactical use of media to intervene in critical contexts, tactical media practitioners drew from Michel de Certeau's theory of tactics as "the arts of the weak."[51] Rather than subsuming tactics to "big picture" strategies as in military culture, de Certeau defines tactics as "a calculated action [within] a terrain imposed on it." That is, this author differentiated tactics from strategies as a question of power relations: those in power delimit a situation through *strategies* that are set to respond to threats and targets. In contrast, "the weak" respond through *tactics*, seizing opportunities "blow by blow," a fact that for de Certeau enables constant mobility and a productive openness to chance.[52]

Tactical media practitioners claim that their aim is not to produce revolutionary processes, as these may be drastically repressed or co-opted by regimes of hegemonic power, or may become themselves totalizing formations. Rather, tactical media practices create disturbances that open fields of possibility. In that sense, tactical media practitioners are "always on the move"; they enact a refusal to become strategic, while recognizing that flexibility and fluidity are also instrumental to late capitalism.[53]

As tactical media works, the EDT's virtual sit-ins and 404 error messages valorize the ephemeral and experimental as activist methods. These methods are based on the open-ended, contingent workings of performance and digital networking as processual tools. In this sense, the EDT's digital incidents update the politics of performance defined by Elin Diamond as "a doing and a thing done," that is, as an embodied transformation of social orders that hegemonic systems present as stable and unchangeable.[54] As performance scholar Joshua Chambers-Letson argues in his study of legal performativity in processes of Asian American racialization, it is precisely "the indeterminacy of the aesthetic encounter" that makes aesthetic performances the primary medium for disrupting political and legal subjection.[55]

These approaches to assessing the efficacy of performance as a tactical resource align with the theory of networks discussed earlier as platforms of control and resistance. Network protocols solidify social orders and structures of domination and appear (and are enforced) as unchangeable. However, while capitalist networks foster pragmatic, controllable, hegemonic uses of the internet, actions such as the EDT's 404 File Not Found open network exchanges to contingency, using established protocols tactically, as a method for "the weak" to seize opportunities. Through performance constellations of convergence of that which is strategically kept separated and contained, the EDT exploits networks as counterhegemonic, relational fields creating a collective disturbance of "the network-as-is."

As I mentioned earlier, another way of assessing the EDT's work is by approaching it as theater, especially since the group uses theater as part of its specific approach to electronic disturbance. Locating the aesthetic mechanisms of virtual sit-ins within a larger structure that is as important as the actual *event* of remote synchronic participation, Dominguez states,

Each performance has a very traditional three-act structure: act 1, the e-mail call to a core actor/audience network (you may also start to get responses from reporters for information and updates); act 2, the *gesture* itself, which is not very interesting to look at since you don't really see that much—you just click (click=action); act three, you re-encounter your core actor/audience network to determine what might have occurred within your staging space, how many people participated, where they came from, what they might have said, and of course what has been reported about the performance. What you want from the performance is a side-loading of the information that creates ripples that add to a much deeper question around the issue that you are documenting in a lived manner via a staged simulation.[56]

In this statement Dominguez demonstrates the intertwined relationship between "traditional" theater poetics (three-act structure) and digital performance (network, side-loading) that is part of the group's tactical use of participatory performance. Using terms such as "side-loading" and "ripples," Dominguez highlights the instrumental role of participatory performance to turn the dissemination of information about a conflict into a performative intervention.

Moreover, Dominguez's use of the concept of *gesture* to characterize the function of the actual virtual sit-in performance works as a hinge between divergent understandings of embodied tactics as didactic, critical, and interventionist, providing another entry point for a critical assessment of the efficacy of the EDT's practices. Dominguez's writing is populated with the concept of gesture, a concept that links his previous work as a theater practitioner to his incursion into digital activism and tactical media:

The notion of "gesture" that I have been playing with as a way to frame different trajectories of performance from my CAE [Critical Art Ensemble] work to EDT and beyond is based on my early encounter as an actor [with] Brecht's idea of "gestus." The "gestus" allows the actors' somatic architecture to comment on the economies of stage, the character event, and the audience as part of the performance itself, while at the same time allowing a fictional narrative to become part of the dialectical de-framing of the social fictions of command and control beyond the theater doors.[57]

The Brechtian concept of *gestus*, as Dominguez reminds us, points to a use of the body, or "somatic architecture," that transcends mere expressivity in order to produce embodied social commentary. Walter Benjamin states that in Brecht's theater, actors do not embody roles but "make inventories," using gesture as a framing device to facilitate the analysis of the behavior and choices of the play's characters.[58] Thus, gestic theater becomes "epic theater," that is, theater as a public forum in which the audience is not driven to *feel*, as epitomized by Greek cathartic drama, but to *think* and to reflect. The efficacy of Brecht's use of *gestus* is that, by aesthetically decomposing a character into a set of behaviors, he portrays society as dynamic and changeable.

On the internet, virtual sit-ins and other forms of networked disruption conceived by Dominguez as gestures illuminate the locales and social relations obscured by the abstract logics of transnational, informational capitalism. Virtual sit-ins and 404 File Not Found actions are "gestic" insofar as they interrupt hegemonic protocols of exchange based on consumerism and consensus. They call attention to the workings of neoliberal exploitation and extractivism on populations not accounted for within smooth capitalist flow and neoliberal calculations.

In this sense, Brecht's theater and the EDT's digital actions or gestures exemplify D. Soyini Madison's definition of performance as a tool that "aims to delve into the undercurrents, the deep particularities, to ask: How is it what it is?"[59] Turning information dissemination about the Zapatista struggle in Chiapas into a collective engagement with networks as sites of control and resistance, the EDT's digital performances provided participants with an embodied method to investigate the "how" and the "what." And to approach the *how*, the processes through which *what is* came to be, as something to be disrupted and potentially transformed. The participatory aspects of virtual sit-ins push these digital performances beyond the distanced intellectual criticality at play within Brechtian theater. Virtual sit-ins and 404 Not Found performances, rather, resonate with Augusto Boal's Forum Theatre and with Boal's recasting of audiences as "spect-actors" who interrupt and modify scenes of oppression developed as part of a rehearsal for radical social transformation.[60]

Participatory performances that mobilize creativity toward political ends, such as the EDT's digital actions, have been met with skepticism by art critics such as Claire Bishop and Jen Harvie. Bishop defines participatory performance as an "art of action interfacing with reality"[61] that she, like Harvie, frames as complacent with neoliberal constructions of self-sufficient, responsible individuals that are promoted to compensate for the state's withdrawal from social provisions. To this issue, Harvie adds questions about the quality and duration of engagement of now-trendy, socially turned performances that emphasize output over artistically informed and sustained activism.[62]

Even though it is difficult to assess how much the EDT's virtual sit-in or 404 Not Found performance participants learned or cared about the Zapatistas, the map I laid out in this chapter about the EDT's origins and its reliance on online and offline activist networks evidences that these are not the kind of performances Bishop and Harvie are concerned about in their legitimate critiques of participatory art. Part of a broader constellation of traditional and emerging tactics, the EDT's digital performances are what queer-of-color performance scholar José Esteban Muñoz calls "tales of historical becoming" that act upon the actual conditions of the present, materializing the opening of a horizon.[63] In their very unfolding, as acts of ephemeral synchronic convergence, the EDT's practices of electronic civil disobedience facilitated symbolic interactions that expanded the repertoire of dissent. As events of disruption and emergence, the EDT's virtual sit-ins materialized worldmaking gestures that critically supplemented transnational movements countering global capital in its multisited, nomadic configurations.

BUILDING A WORLD WHERE MANY FIT

On May 25, 2014, twenty years after the Zapatista insurgence, Subcomandante Marcos announced that he was stepping down. In a public event organized to pay homage to Galeano, a teacher who had been assassinated by paramilitary forces in Chiapas, Marcos announced that he would be *taking in* Galeano's place after the Zapatistas had determined that someone needed to die so that Galeano could live.[64] After five years of absence from the public eye, in a classic Zapatista-style speech, Marcos defined himself as a hologram, a media tactic, and stated that his work was done. Taking Galeano's place so that he could live on, Marcos signaled that the Escuelas Zapatistas and the autonomous projects developed by the indigenous communities in Chiapas are now more crucial to their sustenance and survival than media attention and transnational networking.

Marcos's speech shows that what is important is not what social movement tactics accomplish but, rather, their role within *sustained* processes of social transformation. As part of a multiplicity of tactics, the EDT's online protests constitute paradigmatic examples of how performance as an embodied tool is translated or transmediated to supposedly "disembodied" digital platforms. Through participatory performances in support of the Zapatista struggle, the EDT put in practice technologically mediated notions of embodiment beyond actual bodies.

Conceived as tactics of electronic civil disobedience, in virtual sit-ins the copresence of performers and spectators that defines performance as a body-to-body means of communication was creatively reconfigured to confront contemporary power formations that are networked, transnational, and abstract. As performance constellations of convergence, virtual sit-ins redefined remote spectators as active participants and digital networks as coperformers. Rather than being marginal to performance, in the EDT's online actions, networks enabled the experience of participatory spectatorship that is central to this aesthetic practice, creating convergence out of spatial dislocation.

Just as the Zapatistas used performance and discursive practices to recast the image of the "invisible Indian" into a fully embodied political agent, thus disrupting racist colonial legacies and magnifying their voice, so the EDT employed symbolic performance to mobilize international solidarity as a tangible, collective presence online. These digital actions successfully materialized new ways of performing embodied acts that keep up with the scale and scope of a changing political scenario, and they also taught us new understandings of political efficacy and ways to grasp the significance of digitally mediated collective forms in a highly connected and yet socially fragmented world.

These are all ways in which the straightforward understanding of tactics as means toward an end and as calculated rationality are complicated via nonlinear approaches that embrace the multiplicity, instability, and complexity of performance constellations.[65] This mode of thinking leads performance away from its associations with making and execution and toward performance as an event that engages virtualities and potentialities. This signals a way of disrupting "politics-as-is"[66] in order to open social transformation beyond the horizon of revolution and systemic change as the only valid parameters of accomplishment.

TWO | Articulating Local and
Global Resistance

*Fugitive Capital and On-/Offline Protests
in Argentina*

The changes resisted by communities such as the Zapatistas in the mid-nineties challenged populations throughout the world to find the right tactics to deal with the effects of transnational capitalism as they became widespread. Whereas in the midnineties digital activists argued that street protests had lost efficacy, a few years later this claim was refuted by the crowds of antiglobalization activists that traveled to Seattle to block the World Trade Organization (WTO) summit *on site.* By the early 2000s, protesters began intertwining street and online mobilizations to link affected sites and influence policymaking, a process that was consolidated with the use of social media in the cycle of 2011 protests worldwide.

In cases such as the email campaign *Argentina2001.ppt* discussed here, networked tactics enabled local activists to warn global audiences that economic crises were no longer isolated, containable events specific to local resource mismanagement. Years before the 2008 global financial meltdown, Argentine activists denounced the complicity between international lending institutions, local governments, and speculative investment systems as the root of the economic debacle that broke out in December 2001. The online dissemination of images of pots-and-pans protests, or *cacerolazos,* making international banks accountable for the capital flight that catapulted the crisis, inspired global cacerolazos coordinated through platforms such as Indymedia.[1] Whereas Indymedia was used to coordinate global cacerolazos, websites such as http://www.cacerolazo.com sought to replicate the experience of street protests in virtual space, allowing those with access to the internet to share their grievances and news about grassroots events in their communities.

This chapter focuses on the intertwining of on- and offline responses to the Argentine 2001 economic crisis. In the context of the economic collapse that followed years of deindustrialization and an abrupt capital flight, activists developed digitally networked tactics to "stream out" insurgent street acts and thus create performance constellations connecting local and global resistance to transnational systems of power. This outward swirl of contentious acts contributed key networking tactics to the Argentine "movement of movements." This is how activist and writer Marina Sitrin refers to the local conglomerate of direct-action projects that made Argentina one of the most energetic sites of antiglobalization resistance in the early 2000s.[2] Stream-out performance constellations gave a transnational dimension to the grassroots projects and street protests through which protesters voiced their demands to the state, created spaces of radical democracy, and challenged the hegemony of Washington-based institutions, banks, and financial networks. These on-/offline entanglements galvanized the global justice movement beyond deliberative meetings at the World Social Forum and disruptive events at WTO summits.[3] They amplified spaces and tactics of intervention through which those who adopted emerging political positionings such as "neighbor," "customer," and "internet user-cum-activist" could respond to changes in governing bodies and financial institutions.

Online practices of information dissemination and protest activation exemplify local-to-global tactics directed to denounce the effects of macroeconomic policies on local communities. These practices through which protesters streamed out local resistance to global audiences use the digital against the logic of abstraction, detachment, and decontextualization that benefits capital flow and financial gain.[4] Stream-out performance constellations, pieced together through practices of citizen journalism, digital storytelling, and asynchronous assembly, allowed protesters to create multisited protest performances that built up transnational energy while responding to local specificities. If virtual sit-ins created an experience of digital convergence from disjointed participation, stream-out performance constellations fostered centrifugal modalities of coalition through multiplied engagement.

As we will see, even though the digital practices that propel stream-out performance constellations do not exploit the performativity of digital networks by disrupting network protocols in the way that virtual sit-ins do, *Argentina2001.ppt* and http://www.cacerolazo.com deploy similar action-oriented communication tactics. However, in contrast to examples of digital activism coordinated by experts such as the EDT, practices such as *Argentina2001.ppt* signify a step toward the "many to many" communication style of social media activism and today's on-/offline dynamic entanglements.

Just as the Zapatistas addressed the world via their communiqués disseminated by alterglobalization activists, in the networked activist pieces I analyze here protesters created performance constellations that entwined local and global scenarios, thus opening spaces for citizens' agency within a fabric of transnational networks that both diminished and relied on state power. These on-/offline tactics that would later be taken up by the so-called occupy-the-squares movements in 2011 expanded traditional repertoires of social mobilization and opened possibilities for building transnational power to challenge predatory finance systems that benefit from neoliberal states' policies of economic deregulation and social control.

IN THE EVENT OF CRISIS:
TRANSNATIONAL GOVERNANCE AND CAPITAL FLIGHT

In December 2001, Argentina collapsed. Adding to skyrocketing unemployment rates due to deindustrialization, the country's economic crisis reached a dramatic point when Finance Minister Domingo Cavallo blocked banks by decree after big investors relocated their money abroad.[5] Cavallo's bank freeze decree, known as *corralito financiero*, or financial playpen, limited withdrawals to 250 Argentine pesos per week (at the time, the equivalent of US$178) because the country had literally "run out of money."

Due to the cash limitation, the decree forced people to use debit or credit cards, allegedly following the example of developed countries. In an interview published in *Página 12*, one of Buenos Aires' main newspapers, Cavallo presented his infamous decree as part of a plan to achieve First World status:

> We might have a Soviet economy for ninety days so that we can have a US economy for thirty years. In every country in the world, bank money circulates through the use of debit cards, credit cards, checks, or financial transfers, and cash withdrawals are only made for small change.[6]

This way of handling the financial deficit obviously excluded social sectors that did not have access to the banking system, that is, the many who worked informal jobs or had small businesses. Mainstream media covered the government's powerless and disoriented attempts to put the economy back on track, and the subsequent conflict with the International Monetary Fund over debt payment. Although most people did not know what the country's risk index technically meant, its public disclosure through media reports, along with wind chill reports, contributed to create the dense atmosphere of impending tragedy that pervaded the citizens' daily routines. The media also reported outbreaks of social upheaval in provinces where hundreds of unemployed people picketed or directly looted supermarkets, facing armed repression from store owners and the police.

In a desperate attempt to control the social turmoil, on December 19 at 10:00 p.m. President Fernando de la Rúa announced a thirty-day state of siege during a televised speech. Enraged by this scene, which bore an uncanny resemblance to the 1976 announcement of the military coup, middle-class citizens disobeyed the president's demobilization mandate. Protesters took to the streets, banging pots and pans to demand the resignation of the finance minister and, later, the resignation of the president himself. Moved by a sentiment that would later get expressed through the protest chant "Que se vayan todos" (Out with them all), people loudly voiced their distrust of public officials who had obediently followed policy instructions from Washington-based institutions such as the International Monetary Fund (IMF) and the World Bank.[7]

By clanging on empty pots and pans, in massive cacerolazos, a form of street demonstration that would quickly become a symbol of antineoliberal sentiment, demonstrators made visible and audible the impact that macroeconomic policies had had on their lives. Through their strident presence, demonstrators demanded to be accounted for as stakeholders in the government's economic decisions.[8] Interpellated by the contagious sound of pots and pans that erupted spontaneously from windows and balconies in response to the president's speech, in Buenos Aires protesters gathered in the central points of various neighborhoods to later converge in Plaza de Mayo, the city's financial, political, and administrative center. However, instead of receiving the iconic balcony salute that made populist leaders such as Juan Domingo Perón and Eva Perón famous around the world, protesters were greeted by faceless, repressive power in the form of tear gas, water hoses, rubber bullets, and, later, real bullets.[9] In these incidents, five protesters were killed by police, the dead totaling thirty-nine throughout the country. The televised image of the third democratic chief of state since the end of the military dictatorship in 1983 fleeing Casa Rosada in a helicopter appeared as a repeat that evoked in people's minds another infamous, rushed exit: former president Isabel Martínez de Perón's 1976 helicopter fleeing on March 24, the day the military junta seized power.

To galvanize global support for the Argentine people, activists circulated images of police repression through email, forums, and listservs,

Figure 2: A man confronts police repression in Plaza de Mayo on December 20, 2001. Photo: Diego Giúdice/AP.

reaching out to networks that had mobilized against corporate capitalism in Seattle and Genoa in 1999 and early 2001 respectively. In New York City, where I had just started my graduate coursework in performance studies, I received emails from friends and strangers sharing news about the *Argentinazo*.[10] From those emails, one image completely captured my attention. The image seems to move in a perpetual present, a continuous replay that resists photographic arrest. The scene shows a young man who wields a makeshift cross to confront a diffused antagonist that the image captures in the shape of smoke. The trail of what seems to be tear gas functions as the synecdoche of neoliberal state power: dissolving, yet repressive. While the young man embodies vulnerability as a symbolic weapon, repressive power is faceless, pervasive, disembodied; while the man is still, rooted to the ground, power is light, atmospheric; while the cross stands for compassion and nonviolence, the menacing cloud represents "order."[11] The man's bodily positioning makes a statement: he is determined to stay. The aerial agent acts as a *no-body* that through its traveling state seeks the general dissolution of the scene: *Clear the zone, nothing to do/see here.*[12]

Scenes like this reached international audiences through the very means that had facilitated the capital flight that prompted the protests. Thus, the diffused trail of state power depicted in the protester's picture evokes fugitive capital. Disseminating images of the protests that made tangible the embodied effects of rapidly outward-moving money, activists symbolically inserted their bodies into the information highways of capital flow that facilitate transnational accumulation. Whereas in the Electronic Disturbance Theater's virtual sit-ins activists disrupted digital protocols to clog transnational capital flow, in the context of the 2001 Argentine crisis, protesters exploited digital networks to challenge the abstract, disembodied calculations of financial institutions and international organizations such as the IMF and the World Bank. In contrast to digital convergence tactics deployed by EDT to concentrate support, in the post-2001 crisis, activists resorted to digital dissemination tactics to foster and link distant protests, thus exploiting transnational synergies through outward performance constellations.

DISSOLVING BORDERS, BECOMING TRANSNATIONAL

Argentina's 2001 crisis exemplifies how, following 1990s processes of neoliberal globalization, nation-states minimized regulations to favor transnational trade while increasing their repressive role to curtail social dissent. These processes, however, did not start in the 1990s when neoliberalism became a buzzword attached to "modernization," "First Worldness," "development," and "choice." In countries such as Argentina and Chile, the foundations of deregulated, market-oriented economies were laid during the period of military rule that started in the early 1970s.[13] International lending institutions such as the IMF and the World Bank were crucial actors in setting the ground for the neoliberal turn. These institutions shaped local, economic policies using indebtedness as a tool of social control and to facilitate financial circulation and valorization through deregulated market transactions.

The transformation of the world into an international financial market began in 1870 with Britain in the role of major financier. The First World War weakened European governments and, thus, the United States took on the role of providing financial funds until the 1929 crisis. Between 1947 and 1985, a period that Robert Gilpin identifies as the third and final phase in the process of global financialization, New York became "the international financial centre, the clearing house, the banker for foreign reserves, the main capital market and the lender-of-last-resort."[14] This third face in the transnationalization of financial power was marked by a key event: the 1944 Bretton Woods agreement that tied the value of the dollar to that of gold, and created the IMF and the World Bank as institutions of fiscal management whose role would be to monitor inflation and exchange rates within a context of increasing global commerce.[15] In the post–World War II context of economic reconstruction, the IMF and the World Bank, both tied to the United Nations, granted loans to developing countries. Whereas Washington, DC, became the center for governmental loan-granting and management, New York City emerged as the international finance center for private capital. Thus, in this period the United States consolidated as a global power based on technological development, mass production systems, and military capacity.[16]

Argentina partnered with the IMF in 1956, requesting its first loan for US$75,000 in 1957.[17] As an example of the set of premises that the English economist John Williamson would characterize in 1989 as "the Washington Consensus," in the late 1950s the IMF made this loan conditional upon deficit reduction, budget cuts, and the liberalization of the economy. As in neighboring Chile, in Argentina the deregulation of the economy took place through violent tactics of policy implementation, particularly targeting workers and union leaders who resisted the erasure of labor rights and unions.

The military, which ruled Argentina from 1976 to 1983, played a crucial role in this process, eliminating laws that protected workers to favor capital. Besides the now well-known human rights violations perpetrated by different branches of the armed forces against political dissidents—many of whom were "disappeared" in clandestine detention centers and are still missing—Finance Minister Alfredo Martínez de Hoz, who served between 1976 and 1981, carried out a plan that would rapidly transform Argentina into a financial economy. Whereas the military government cut wages and social welfare provisions, and eliminated dissidents, the finance ministry offered high interest rates to incentivize investors who subsequently moved their money in and out of the country following their assessment of the country's stability. As a result, many factories went bankrupt due to the lack of operating funds and the high costs of credit and indebtedness in an economic system that favored speculative, financial capital.[18] Additionally, Argentina's sovereign debt increased during the dictatorship due to the nationalization of private debt in 1982, when the state assumed responsibility for privately acquired debt.

In the 1990s, in debt-ridden Argentina President Carlos Menem promoted the intensive application of the Washington Consensus as a way of grappling with the country's financial burden and as a path toward an American way of life that the population had consumed via cultural imperialism.[19] Budget cuts, the liberalization of the financial market, the privatization of state-owned companies, and the further erosion of employment regulations were some of the policy changes implemented by Menem, who had centered his campaign on the promise of a "productive revolution." The official implementation of the Washington Consensus in the 1990s was thus the final step in a process that had been initiated during the military dictatorship.

In 2001, when the pronounced economic and social crisis that had been developing since the midnineties became evident and widespread, those deprived of their jobs, their savings, and their trust in local government directed their attention to the IMF, whose policy recommendations had been dutifully followed by local elected officials. The aforementioned pots-and-pans demonstrations were the most immediate response to the December 2001 collapse of the Argentine economy. However, unemployed workers throughout the country had long been signaling the economy's freefall when they started blocking roads in the midnineties.[20] *Piquetes*, or road blockades, the main tactic of what became the *piquetero* movement, allowed those no longer able to stop production in their workplace an opportunity to disrupt the flow of capital by blocking routes and roads and thus draw mass media's attention to abandoned towns.[21]

Other grassroots projects such as the worker-run factories movement and the neighborhood assemblies sought to respond to critical needs in a context of cash shortages and political distrust. These projects undid the politics of individualism promoted by neoliberal approaches that foreground entrepreneurship and meritocracy instead of social justice as self-managed solutions to structural problems. In a moment in which the political class was challenged through slogans such as "Out with them all," protesters assembled to create instances of direct democracy that Colectivo Situaciones defines as "nuevo protagonismo" (new protagonism). This term characterizes transversal forms of organizing and decision-making that replaced delegative, partisan politics.[22] Collective, cooperative experiments of new protagonism resonated with the grassroots practices of good government promulgated by the Zapatistas.[23]

Along with the groups defined by a working-class agenda, some of the nodes that shaped the nonhierarchical movement of social networks in Argentina were organized by middle-class sectors, such as the *ahorristas* (bank customers), who were affected by the government's decision to freeze bank accounts and devalue the peso. The *corralito* decree turned bank customers into enraged protesters who gathered in front of bank premises and carried out loud cacerolazos. One of the traces of these cacerolazos, a graffito that circulated on the internet, captures the group's sentiment toward transnational banking and investment:

SPECIAL OFFER:
YOU DEPOSIT DOLLARS AND
WE GIVE YOU SHIT IN RETURN.[24]

The events of December 2001 and the subsequent popular mobilizations and grassroots projects posed a challenge for artists who had to rethink the role of cultural production in such a context of social turmoil. Many artist collectives such as TPS (Taller Popular de Serigrafía, or Popular Silk Screen Workshop), GAC (Grupo de Arte Callejero, or Street Art Group), and Colectivo Etcétera (Etcetera Collective) worked side by side with social movements in pickets, occupied factories, and in neighborhood assemblies, contributing crucial tools to fight evictions, connect struggles, and give visibility to specific conflicts.[25]

In their article "En Brukman se cosen las redes sociales" (Social networks sown at Brukman) published on *Página 12* on November 10, 2003, activist Mabel Bellucci and TPS member Karina Granieri chronicle how Brukman workers were able to keep their job posts by turning the bankrupt garment factory into a worker-run cooperative. Bellucci and Granieri celebrate the factory's expropriation in favor of the workers, recalling how artists, activists, and social movements turned the factory into "a territory of rehearsals and explorations of spontaneous and self-managed modalities of political intervention."[26] One of these interventions took place when workers, the majority of whom were women, were evicted from Brukman in April 2003 after sustaining their occupation for over a year. Collaborating with the workers, artist collectives and activists organized what they called a *maquinazo*, a sort of "sewing machine picket line" that turned an activity usually considered domestic and docile into a combative act. Operating sewing machines donated by neighbors, the evicted Brukman workers cordoned the factory and made clothes for the victims of a recent flood in the province of Santa Fe. Silk screen artists from TPS stamped clothes with images representing the Brukman workers' struggle. Before the height of social media, artists, activists, and mobilized workers in postcrisis Argentina used performance to create networks that exploited the synergy between material and symbolic production to build power and combat the effects of engineered crises.

These collaborations can be placed as part of Latin American genealogies of community-based artistic practice and collective creation (*creación colectiva*), conceptualized in Anglo-Saxon contexts as social art practice or socially engaged art.[27] Art historian Andrea Giunta states that the postcrisis period, which she locates between 2001 and 2004, was marked by "the aura of solidarity."[28] Giunta claims that through their collaboration with social movements artists sought to legitimize their social role within the climate of distrust that pervaded Argentine society, affecting politicians, intellectuals, and artists alike.

In contrast with Giunta's skeptical position, Latin American scholar Jean Graham-Jones argues that cultural productions added an important node to the movement of movements that experimented with forms of social reproduction and political intervention beyond the antagonistic logic of street protests. In her contribution to the debate on the role of art during the crisis, Graham-Jones locates theater productions as part of broader art-activist mechanisms that countered neoliberal individualism through the "production of collectivity." Graham-Jones contends that in a context of socioeconomic collapse, cultural production became a crucial platform of survival and recovery through the reconstitution of identity.[29]

Besides participating in on-the-ground projects such as worker-run factories and art-activist collaborations linking local movements, activists resorted to new tools to amplify and replicate collective actions, addressing and responding to local and transnational power systems. Through digitally networked tactics, activists configured performance constellations that streamed out local mobilization tactics to global audiences, both to generate support and to connect sites of neoliberal crises and resistance. Digital networks not only facilitated global mobilization but propelled the constellative impetus of new social movements.[30] Though, in the past, movements have also built coalitional relations to share resources or interlink agendas, digital networks have intensified this modality of clustering that connects different forms of collective mobilization without subsuming them under a totalizing structure or identity.

CREATING LOCAL-TO-GLOBAL CONSTELLATIONS: STREAMING OUT PROTEST

Although much has been written about on-the-ground movements in post-2001 Argentina, digital tactics have received very little attention, despite their key function in connecting local mobilizations to the antiglobalization movement that had recently converged in Seattle, reinvigorating the case for street protest, now with a digital spin.[31] In cases such as those that we will explore in this section, internet users experimented with communication tactics that sought to reproduce the affective appeal of street protests to actively engage audiences. These practices reworked the dominant digital paradigm of discreteness, separation, and decontextualization that favors capitalism, and financial speculation specifically, into a medium for bridging local and global scales of resistance.

For example, online platforms such as Indymedia.org, an open publishing network launched by the Independent Media Center right before the 1999 Seattle protests, enabled activists to mobilize globally, expanding ephemeral street demonstrations. As a precursor of today's social media activism, this platform allowed media activists to post street-level documentation of protests, bypassing mainstream media censorship or misreporting through the practice of citizen journalism. Additionally, through Indymedia's discussion features, users were able to coordinate multisited protests. This shows the platform's alignment with legacies of community organizing and the then-emergent open-source movement. In the context of post-2001 Argentina, contributors used Indymedia to spread news of pots-and-pans protests so that, as their analog referents do sonically, they would draw supporters in and accumulate dissent through physical and virtual spatial entanglements.

In ways that foreground the meaning of communication as the "making common to many," projects like Indymedia transferred the ideals of radical democracy enacted in assemblies and cooperative production sites to media platforms.[32] Even though the digital divide is definitely a factor we need to consider when assessing which bodies were part of internet activism in the early 2000s, digital networks were a crucial asset in activists' efforts to frame the Argentine crisis as more than a local mismanagement of resources.

However, as John Hammond and others claim, in the context of global activism, when many simply lacked digital access, resources, or skills, online mobilization could potentially broaden the gap between North and South.[33] Additionally, the ease of communication enabled by digital tools often creates information overflow (as is usually the case in social media), and this threatens to subtract necessary energy from long-term organizing. Nevertheless, as Hammond himself notes, the way to address these challenges is not to do away with these tools but to acknowledge their limitations and complement digital tactics (or entangle them, as I advocate here) with other tactics and resources.[34]

Whereas Indymedia was predominantly used by antiglobalization activists and journalists, local protesters used email to reach out to local and transnational audiences not necessarily assembled in preestablished networks. For example, the picture of the demonstrator in Plaza de Mayo that I discussed earlier was part of a PowerPoint presentation disseminated by email on January 2002. Named *Argentina2001.ppt*, the piece employs the linear slide presentation to explain the crisis in the style of a step-by-step cooking recipe. In fifty-six slides the presentation teaches readers what it took to build "the bomb" that caused the December *estallido* (blast), a term used to refer to the economic, political, and social effects of the crisis. In the aftermath of the 9/11 terrorist attacks on the World Trade Center, *Argentina2001.ppt* deploys the "ticking bomb" scenario to denounce the political and economic practices that created a volatile, hazardous environment, whose worldwide effects became painfully clear with the 2008 global economic meltdown.

Against a black background the narrative unfolds slide by slide thusly:

Did you ever stop to think what's in a bomb?
Do you want to see an explosive combination?
Take note:
First: four years of recession.
Second: 40 percent of the population is unemployed and has no
    prospects.
Third: 14,500,000 people below the poverty line in a population of
    37,000,000.
Slowly add: A puppet president that passes unpopular legislation.
Let simmer during a year and four months.
Finally, stir all of the above energetically and add
    a sinister finance minister, a liar, an insensitive, paranoid, and
    "an all-powerful man"[35] who devours a complicit parliament
    and squanders reserves under the shadow of the International
    Monetary Fund (IMF).
The result will be an unstable, starving population and a highly
    explosive country.[36]

The slideshow uses a processual narrative structure presenting the crisis as a manufactured rather than accidental event that had been long in the making. Through questions and instructions ("Do you want to see an explosive combination?" and "Take note") the PowerPoint piece engages readers as active interlocutors in the act of learning about the particulars of a crisis,

not only as witnesses but also as potential protagonists. A manually operated slideshow might seem a weak form of interactivity; however, *Argen-
tina2001.ppt* presents a compelling approach to information dissemination
and/as a call to action, especially when compared to today's activist use of
animated GIFs to quickly deliver information about a cause.

After laying out the "ingredients" or conditions that precipitated the
crisis, *Argentina2001.ppt* changes the cooking recipe for a chronology.[37] The
presentation proceeds to narrate the events of December 19 and 20, focusing on pots-and-pans demonstrations as the main method through which
protesters provoked "the fall of the system." The slideshow does not, however, postulate that the story is over. In a manner that highlights the cycli-
cal nature of economic crises (and the equally iterative character of protest
repertoires) the narrator states that, if abuses go on, the pots and pans will
be banged on again. In the face of citizens' distrust in representative democracy, *Argentina2011.ppt* foregrounds pots and pans, and the dissonant collective assembly they generated, as the main instrument for asserting citizens' agency beyond electoral polls. Here, pots-and-pans protests are
evoked as a popular impeachment tool, a form of participatory politics that
complemented assemblies and other direct action projects.[38]

The act of email forwarding by those who received the PowerPoint presentation in their mailboxes constitutes another important aspect of this
digital intervention that engages participants in performance constellations beyond information dissemination. In a way that resembles the
"human mic"—the body-based method of assembly communication
employed by the Occupy Wall Street movement to circumvent sound
amplification regulations during their gatherings in Zucotti Park in 2011—
email forwarding functioned as a technology of participatory enunciation.
Through this gesture, email senders demonstrated their belonging to a collective. As visual theorists Jimena Durán Prieto and Esteban Javier Rico
claim, through the iterative performance of forwarding, senders ratified
the legitimacy of the protests, transforming an anonymous cultural artifact
(the PowerPoint file) into a collective narrative.[39] This transfer from one
sender to others did not deprive people of their possessions as capital flight
did; instead, it configured plural alignment. *Argentina2001.ppt* thus transformed one-to-one information transmission into a networked process that
brought forth an asynchronous and dispersed collective, further facilitating local-global networks of dissent and alliance.

Whereas *Argentina2001.ppt* created stream-out performance constellations by engaging readers through digital storytelling and forwarding,
other digitally mediated activist productions, such as the now defunct

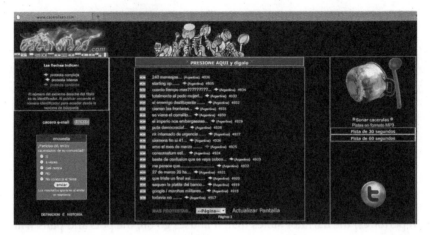

Figure 3: Pots-and-pans web forum.

site http://www.cacerolazo.com, engaged visitors by simulating the experience of the street cacerolazo. This site was in essence a web forum allowing people to post comments about assemblies, barter clubs, and protests.
When visitors landed on the home page, they were welcomed by an animated image of a spoon banging on a pot accompanied by the corresponding sound.

A hyperlink reading "presione aquí y dígalo" (click here and say it)
took users to the forum section of the website, where they were able to post
their demands or announce upcoming street mobilizations or events.
Online users were invited to enhance their experience by clicking on MP3
files that reproduced various versions of the strident sound of pots and
pans. Images of flags representing Latin American countries and Spain
framed the protest as a translocal phenomenon that could be joined by protesters in other countries.

Although physical bodies were not part of this cacerolazo, http://www.
cacerolazo.com sought to recreate and sustain the atmosphere of social unrest
that prompted street pots-and-pans as outbursts connecting domestic and
public space, that is, individual and shared conditions. In the online cacerolazo, users not only read and posted calls to action; by clicking on the audio
files, they activated the nonlinguistic layer that defines cacerolazos as protests built on symbolic, expressive, and tactical noise. Using features such as
animated graphics and MP3 audio files, http://www.cacerolazo.com sought to
reconstruct the physically grounded experience that turns individual noise
into a growing indignant cacophony. One could say, however, that in con-

trast to street cacerolazos as cumulative bodily performances, the digital cacerolazo was a solitary happening. Yet if we consider that in 2001 many people surfed the web in *locutorios*, or cybercafes, the notion of the online cacerolazo as a solitary desktop protest gets complicated as people in the cybercafe would hear the MP3 file and maybe be compelled to address strangers about the country's situation and/or join ongoing street mobilizations.

Operation Vocalize, a video posted by Anonymous on YouTube during the emergence of the Occupy Wall Street movement in late October 2011, supports this speculation, providing an approach to online cacerolazos as productive tools in their own right, particularly when protesters are not able to demonstrate in state or privately regulated spaces. The video's accompanying text reads:

> If you don't want to go on the streets or [you are] not able to, practice the Cacerolazo tactic, which is playing loud chants off speakers or making noise from your own house. This tactic [has] proven successful in other countries; it's time to put it to good use, here, and everywhere else.[40]

Although online cacerolazos and playing "loud chants off speakers" alone would perhaps not be as effective as street cacerolazos, by teaching to Occupy Wall Street demonstrators a practice that became a staple of resistance to neoliberal policies, Anonymous drew a performatic connection, a performance constellation, that linked sites affected by transnational economic policies by entangling on-/offline aural tactics and private and public spaces.[41] Referencing the cacerolazo as a proven tactic, as a way of "vocalizing" collective rejection and challenging abusive hegemonic systems, Anonymous provided a performative prompter that could potentially expand the Occupy movement beyond its confines and limitations. More importantly, it located Occupy within a broader history of economic crises that prefigured the 2008 global meltdown.[42]

Like virtual sit-ins, digital storytelling and online cacerolazos as asynchronous assembly tactics engaged online audience's kinesthetic imagination to generate an experience of copresence and thus build networked power in multisited protest sites. Whereas EDT's virtual sit-ins relied on durational synchronic participation, *Argentina2001.ppt* and online cacerolazos used personal interpellation ("Do you want to see an explosive combination?" "click here and say it") employing interactivity to turn an asynchronic encounter into a simulated real-time mobilization.

If on- and offline mobilization in the context of the Argentine crisis sought to reach out to transnational audiences, highlighting the concrete effects of abstract financial operations to spark global solidarity, offline demonstrations, such as the Waksteins' in-bank holiday analyzed next, generated opportunities for affected people to engage transnational financial flows in physical space. Even though this protest performance does not have a "stream-out" impetus like pots-and-pans and digitally networked tactics, it also engages with capital fugitivity, working against strategies of decontextualization and abstraction at the intersection between intangible capital and concrete bodies. As an example of what sociologist Horacio González calls "the uncertain but effective pedagogy of extended individuals,"[43] the Waksteins' in-bank vacation can be conceptualized as a "bring-in" performance constellation that opens a frictive encounter between body-based tactics aimed toward social mobility, and networked, out-bound strategies fostering capitalist accumulation.

REVERSING THE CURRENT: *VACACIONES EN EL BANCO*

Dance theorist Randy Martin states that financial instruments such as derivatives "abstract capital from its body."[44] Martin explains that, whereas assembly line production involved a process of fragmentary effort that resulted in a commodity that was more than the sum of its parts (think, for example, a car), what Martin calls "financial engineering" follows the opposite process of productive, profitable disassembly. As a money form exchangeable in global markets, derivatives are dispersed attributes detached from commodities and reassembled with elements from other commodities, bearing more value as *derivatives* than as part of their original sources. Like currency exchange or interest rates, derivatives exemplify mutating forms of financial gain and loss that include events that may or may not happen (like weather-related catastrophes) as conditions that impact valorization.

In the context of the 2001 financial collapse, those affected by capital flight and by a longer cycle of processes that uprooted capital from industrial production responded to the dispersed logic of financial capitalism with a contrarian logic, using site-specific performance to symbolically *reattach* capital to bodies and life projects. Protest performances such as *Vacaciones en el banco* (In-bank holiday) reversed the stream of capital flight facilitated by digital capitalism by disrupting on-site banking operations through a scene that sought to leverage protesters' resources vis-à-vis transnational investment networks.

Vacaciones en el banco, a protest performance carried out by a middle-class family in the lobby of an HSBC bank branch in Buenos Aires, illustrates the use of body-based tactics as a tool employed by those affected by the 2001 capital flight to transform a situation of vulnerability into a space of contestation.[45] At the beginning of December 2001, after a massive capital flight emptied 25 percent of banks' deposits, Finance Minister Cavallo froze bank accounts and limited withdrawals. The government's bank freeze was allegedly implemented to guarantee the continuity of the convertibility plan that had pegged the peso to the US dollar for a period of ten years. As mentioned earlier, mass-media journalists termed the government's blockade of bank accounts *corralito financiero* (financial corral or playpen). The word *corralito*, which initially referred to the severely limited circulation of money, was later used to communicate people's feelings of being physically trapped.[46] The phrase captured the contrast between big investors that were able to transfer their money abroad smoothly and small savings' holders who were struck unexpectedly by the government's bank freeze order.[47]

At the time of the implementation of the bank freeze, the Wakstein family had US$50,000, a sum they had received as part of an inheritance, in a fixed-term deposit. Determined to retrieve the family's savings, Marcelo Wakstein, who worked as a plumber, lined up in his HSBC bank branch three times a week for a period of two hours. One day, complaining about the lack of financial results that compromised his ability to work as an independent contractor and also affected the family's vacation plans, Wakstein and family decided to orchestrate a special appearance on the bank's premises to attract public attention and thus put pressure on the bank's administration to respond. The Waksteins emailed Buenos Aires' main newspapers and television and radio stations to announce their protest performance as a form of public exposé or *escrache* shaming their bank.[48]

On January 24, 2002, on arrival, the family proceeded to spread out their props, framing their live image with a placard reading: "Este banco se quedó con el futuro de mis hijos. Devuélvanselo" (This bank took away my children's future. Give it back).

As anthropologist Diego Zenobi claims, by framing the situation as detrimental to their children's life prospects, the Waksteins transformed a dispute over access to money into a claim about savings and social mobility, a value at the core of middle-class identity.[49] Although the issue of the deferred vacation was the scene's humorous visual leitmotif, the Waksteins strategically chose to focus their claim on their children's compromised future, an issue that would compel many other wronged customers to align

Figure 4: The Wakstein family in their *In-Bank Vacation* protest in Buenos Aires during the 2001–2002 bank freeze. Photo courtesy of Enrique García Medina.

with them, potentially amplifying the action. Confronted with the satirical scene of the family's takeover of the bank, those standing in line burst into laughter and applauded.[50] Because journalists had responded to the email announcing the *escrache*, the Waksteins appeared live on TV in a matter of minutes. The bank's staff reacted immediately and proceeded to evacuate patrons through the parking lot. Trying to avoid a scandal, the bank personnel allowed the family to continue with their protest, now displayed through the windows for an outside audience of reporters and passersby.

The following week, approximately sixty people joined Wakstein and his family in what he considers the first "marcha de los ahorristas estafados" (defrauded bank customers' march).[51] Because this time the family was not allowed to enter the bank, the Waksteins staged the vacation scene and posed for photographers on the bank's steps. Local and international press, including *The Guardian* and *The Telegraph*, covered this ingenious protest for international audiences.[52]

At that time, other desperate bank customers also carried out more extreme actions in banks' premises, such as setting themselves on fire or breaking in with toy guns, in an attempt to make the banks take their demands seriously.[53] There was also another loose group of enraged *ahorristas* who graffitied banks' walls and smashed windows. In response to these actions, the terrified bank authorities bunkered the premises by attaching metallic sheets to the windows.

As tactical behavior, the bank holiday performance transformed the customers' passive, docile waiting into an active appropriation of space that engaged local and nomadic financial networks ("This bank took away . . .") By staging *waiting* as an actively endured action, the Waksteins counteracted the immobilization that the *corralito* decree had subjected customers to. More crucially, through their performative occupation, protesters were able to confront transnational actors by framing the bank freeze as theft.

By holding their savings in US dollars, the Waksteins and other account holders had sought to tame the fear of financial instability that has historically haunted Argentine society after being prey to internationally mandated reforms such as those imposed by the IMF. The convertibility law that had pegged the peso to the dollar for ten years had diminished those fears and created a general atmosphere of confidence. Still, as many critics of the savings holders' protests noted, this policy had devastated other social sectors, a fact that the *piquetero* movement had denounced since the midnineties by blocking roads in remote towns.

Using bodily performance to symbolically reverse the flow of capital, the savings holders' structured occupation of space stood in contrast to the virtual interactions that constitute what Dan Schiller terms "digital capitalism."[54] This term highlights how integral digital networks are to new forms of capitalist accumulation. Sociologist Ignacio Lewkowicz theorizes the transformations at play within digital capitalism through the concept of "transubstantiation."[55] Instead of the term's original use, to describe how Communion wafers and wine are transformed into Christ's body and blood, Lewkowicz's notion of transubstantiation emphasizes how in digital capitalism, money (the body of capitalism as we knew it) turns into informational bytes; it dematerializes. For Lewkowicz, in late capitalism there are two heterogeneous substances at play (money and bytes) and banks operate as the interface between them, facilitating the process of conversion from paper money to information.

Lewkowicz's theory implies that the customers who demonstrated at the banks failed to understand the logic of digital capital; the transubstantiation process renders the bank protests ineffectual: the money is no longer there. As tactical media practitioners stated, this makes streets "dead capital," and physical protests, ineffectual. However, as centripetal, "bringin" performance constellations, protest performances such as the Waksteins' are indeed effective, precisely because they give material form to the disappearance of the money, connecting sites and flows of capital to concrete bodies. By demonstrating at local banks, the Waksteins and the broader savings holders' movement demanded that the international networks that had made the capital flight possible maintain their commitment to local customers. In Argentina, in the 1990s half of the banking sector was internationalized, allegedly so that, in the event of a crisis, the banks' central branches would rescue their local subsidiaries.[56] Nevertheless, post-2001 this did not happen. Rather, banks performed as highways for the relocation of the money to foreign coffers.[57] That is why, although the money was technically *not there*, banks were indeed the appropriate sites at which to protest *and* perform in 2001–2002 Argentina.

Years after the Waksteins' protest performance, in 2010, US satiric activist Reverend Billy enacted a similar "bring-in" operation. During the loan crisis that was part of the 2008 global meltdown, and before the emergence of the Spanish Indignados and Occupy movements, the actor Bill Talen (disguised as Reverend Billy, a Protestant preacher) stormed banks with his Church of Stop Shopping Gospel Choir. They confronted predatory financial political economies by exorcizing ATM machines of "bad loans." In these performances of exorcism as an act of transfer, the expulsion or decoupling of a bad spirit from the purged body intervened in the machinery of financial transfers. This is another example of activists' symbolic tactics drawing together speculative, networked economics and everyday sites and bodies affected by deregulated financial practices. The "bad loan" concept refers to the crisis created through subprime mortgages that epitomized the logic of the derivative investment instrument described by Martin as relying on movement, transfer, detachment, and reattachment.[58] In the United States, mortgage holders and their commitments were reattached to new credit holders under changing conditions. Through this performance, Reverend Billy problematized that coupling and, in a new version of the nonviolent protest tradition, reclaimed ethics for protesters, highlighting the delinquent side of operations usually perceived as impersonal.

Another protest performance that resonates with the Waksteins' protest and their consumer-customer tactics is the performative occupation that members of the Occupy movement carried out against Bank of America (BOA) in March 2012. A small group of protesters carried several pieces of furniture into a BOA branch and installed a living room in the lobby. When approached by the bank's manager, the occupiers explained that the US government's bailout of the bank for a sum of US$230 billion had given them the right, as taxpayers, to move in, particularly after the bank had evicted them from their homes. The video documenting this protest was disseminated on YouTube and other social media sites. Following the action's success, activists set March 15, 2012, as "Move-In Day" for others to replicate the protest at their familiar bank branches. The Move-in Day literalized a previous campaign from November 5, 2011, called "Bank Transfer Day," in which occupiers mobilized account holders to transfer their money to not-for-profit credit unions. The BOA protesters were part of a performance constellation that entangled physical and digital sites of monetary transactions and, by "moving in," they drew attention to the way "move out" investments had left them in the open.[59]

When I interviewed Marcelo Wakstein in 2005, four years after the first *Vacaciones*, he recalled those days and the legal, spectacular, and political actions he and his family performed in response to the bank freeze.[60] He pointed out that one of the things that struck him the most about the effects of their protest performance was that he and his family, who had no activist training, had prompted the bank's closing. "I was so proud. Two people close down the third [ranking] bank of the world."[61] Wakstein's comment shows the tactical force of body-based performance insofar as the mere presence of people at the bank, configured in a spatial arrangement that challenged the docile choreography of standing in line, was enough to disrupt financial operations, even if fleetingly. In the following comment, Wakstein communicates his understanding of the tactical component of the performance:

> The bank's goal is to make money. If you don't let the bank work, it loses money. Well, then, this was our idea: to not let the bank work. We were not able to work because we needed to protest constantly. So not letting the bank work was a way of paying back in kind, with the means we had available to us.[62]

In this statement Wakstein framed his family's vacation performance in economic terms, as a form of payback. The currency used was a disruption of the bank's operations meant to reciprocate the freeze that had immobilized the family after the bank had benefited from capital flow. Thus, *Vacaciones* was not only a witty way of structuring a demand; it was a form of embodied agency used to create a crack in the interface that had facilitated the transubstantiation of money into bytes, a tactic that symbolically reversed the stream of fugitive capital.

STREAMING OUT / BRINGING IN:
NEOLIBERAL ENTANGLEMENTS AND ITS BODIES

As sociologist Elizabeth Jelin explains, social struggle, as the process through which subordinate actors enter sociopolitical space, redefines political space per se, enabling those at the margins to expand their social and political citizenship.[63] Besides ushering in one of the most strenuous times in Argentine history, the crisis of 2001 produced a myriad of forms of radical democracy, contentious tactics, movement coalitions, and transnational organizing. In a country with a long tradition of protest and activism, popular organization, and public space occupation as political pedagogies, the post-2001 era contributed important tools to expand and update protest and social mobilization repertoires.

Although, at first, the Argentine network of protest and activist tactics was celebrated with the motto "Piquete y cacerola, la lucha es una sola" (Picket line and pots-and-pans, the struggle is the same), neighborhood assemblies, pots-and-pans, and bank customers' protests came under scrutiny later. Critics such as Nicolás Casullo and Sebastián Carassai condemned them as mediatic and self-serving endeavors.[64] However, 2001 is today cited by activists as part of their political education and as an important, if complicated, hallmark of local resistance. During her speech in Congress as part of the 2018 debate to decriminalize abortion, feminist activist and journalist María Florencia Alcaraz stated that she and the massive movement for reproductive rights are "the daughters of 2001."[65] Sociologist Graciela Di Marco also cites 2001, particularly the women that were part of the unemployed workers' movements, as a key component of what she calls "a feminist people."[66] What divides critics and advocates is how to understand the motives behind the 2001 mobilization: did all of these movements want something new, or did they want a return to the previous order, to the pre–December 2001 peso-dollar equivalence? In that case, a time when the peso was pegged to the dollar, an "order" that favored those with disposable income, would mean little to those who lost their jobs due to difficult-to-sustain monetary exchange policies.

In 2018, as Argentines were once again faced with news about rapidly developing indebtedness and the IMF's comeback in a context of, yet again, capital flight and high speculation under Mauricio Macri's business-oriented administration, 2001 not only resonates as a cautionary tale but also provides a handy toolbox. Of course, as digital activism tools, Indymedia, PowerPoint presentations, and online cacerolazos are now obsolete and have been replaced by social media. Ubiquitous media technology has accelerated and intensified people's capacity to make their voices heard, coordinate with others, and particularly fight the state-sponsored *blindaje mediático* (media blockage), the equivalent of the financial playpen, this time blocking information to engineer consensus. Through memes, hashtag campaigns, GIFs, and street protests, mobilized sectors contest the status quo and pierce the administration's facade, winning important battles when fired employees are reinstated to their public sector jobs and incendiary policy or legal decisions are reversed due to massive pressure.[67]

The on-/offline protests we focused on here are part of the foundation of these mobilizations and conquests. They provided new tools not only for resisting but also for learning about new world orders ("the parts of the bomb") and about other, more livable, worlds that might be possible. Stream-out and bring-in performance constellations sustained and propelled the 2001 movement of movements beyond its local confines. Performance constellations that articulate street and online actions in synergetic relationships function as a hinge between the digital activism practices of the 1990s and the networked performances of the social media and mobile media era. They demonstrate that, as capital becomes increasingly dematerialized and abstract, bodily performance and digital networking prove crucial for activists and artists to engage with both local and transnational systems of power. In the following chapters we will see how, in addition to fostering the intertwined relationship between the streets and the web, performance constellations also expand the notion of the event of collective action, connecting stylized behavior across temporalities through tactics of endurance and persistence.

| Expanding Moves, Enacting Futurity

Debt Governance, Transmedia Activism, and
the Chilean "Fearless Generation"

It's Friday, June 24, 2011, around 5:30 p.m., and a mass of students take over Plaza de la Constitución, across from the Government Palace in Santiago, Chile. Passersby get their phone cameras ready. This does not look like the kind of protest the city has grown used to in the past month. Suspenseful music starts and Michael Jackson's 1983 hit *Thriller* fills the air. Disguised as zombies wearing different versions of professional garment (lab coats, construction hats, business suits) the students begin their synchronized dance, led by Jackson's surrogate in his memorable red leather jacket. Unlike the decomposing bodies that emerge from marked cemetery plots in *Thriller*'s video, these zombies carry tombstone-shaped signs themselves, displaying a shared story on their chest: "Yo morí debiendo" (I died owing/in debt). Despite the overwhelming presence of this tragic statement multiplied in hundreds of bodies, there is an atmosphere of celebration, a kind of carnivalesque defiance of what the signs present as an anticipated destiny. When the performance is over, the crowd of performers and spectators bursts into applause and shouts of support for this event, which was launched on Facebook the week before.[1] Compelled by the performance, social media users extend the flash mob's "eventness"[2] online, disseminating clips and pictures, thus drawing more people into the student mobilization toward public education.

This chapter analyzes performance constellations of asynchronic cooperation within the 2011 Chilean student movement. During the so-called Chilean Winter, students sustained several months of collective mobilization through traditional forms of activism such as assemblies, rallies, occupations, and innovative protest performances coordinated and disseminated online. In protest performances such as the zombie flash mob *Thriller por la educación* (Thriller for education) and the relay run *1800 horas por la educación* (1,800 hours for education) student organizers choreographed street collective action, inciting supporters to join the performance on-the-ground and/or to make it reverberate online.[3] Through these asynchronous performance constellations that mobilized participants' concerted action across discontinuous temporalities, students challenged the government's approach to education as a matter of individual financial investment rather than citizens' rights. Occupying physical and virtual space through corporeal and temporal arrangements that defied urban protocols, students contested the hegemony of "debt time" as a technique of neoliberal subjectivation and control.

Like the Electronic Disturbance Theater's virtual sit-ins, *Thriller for education* and *1,800 Hours for education* relied on experiences of liveness and copresence as crucial components of collective action. In these protest performances, the online dissemination of street events was not merely reproductive but generative. The dialectical relationship between on- and offline mobilization thus shook up the traditional hierarchy of face-to-face, "unmediated" live performance over the mediated, recorded broadcast. In these examples, the eventness of performance, that is, the affective force of live performance previously defined by the spatial and temporal copresence between performers and spectators, was enhanced by the performance's circulation online. Thus protest performances became distributed events articulated in performance constellations of noncontiguous cooperation between participants.

The entanglement between street protests and their online reverberations enabled activists to expand their movement, reaching those who had been apathetic or hesitant to join collective acts of dissent in the past.[4] Relying on different modalities of collective performance as tactics of sustained and expanded affective engagement, Chilean activists and supporters mobilized vital responses to biopolitical modes of capitalist extraction such as personal indebtedness. They contested debt governance's hold on bodies and temporality, bringing forth opportunities for sustained civic engagement in the extended "now" of performance constellations.

DEBT TIME:
TRANSFORMING EDUCATION RIGHTS INTO THE RIGHT TO CREDIT

The Chilean student protests of 2011 made visible the population's rejection of the increasing social inequality caused by a political economic system inherited from Augusto Pinochet's dictatorship (1973–1990).[5] In the field of education, processes of neoliberalization were carried out as part of

a 1979 structural reform called "Siete modernizaciones" (Seven moderniza-
tions).[6] The program applied market logics to the educational system, causing a deep fragmentation in civil society.[7] Leaving Pinochet's system in
place, in the early 2000s democratic president Ricardo Lagos Escobar from
the coalition of center-left parties called La Concertación implemented a
scholarship program, allegedly to guarantee access to education to the
poorest sectors of the Chilean middle class. This system of scholarships
actually resulted in a government-backed credit plan that was later revealed
to have mainly benefited the banking sector, leaving graduates in serious
debt. Moreover, the high school charter program and voucher plan through
which the state partially subsidized families' choices within a marketplace
approach to education resulted in an "educational ghetto," due to the
state's defunding of public institutions.[8]

Frustrated with La Concertación's continuation of a system from Pinochet's regime, the 2011 wave of student protests urged the government of
right-wing president Sebastián Piñera to launch a program of far-reaching
reforms. Through their representatives and through street demonstrations the
students demanded that the state guarantee free, public, high-quality education. Mobilized students also called for structures of regulation and control,
plurality in decision-making processes, and intercultural inclusion and inte-
gration.[9] This last point sought to address the fact that the government's
defunding of public education had transformed it into a class-based system
that severely segregated low-income and marginalized students, particularly
Mapuche students. Overall, the student protests urged the end of the myth of
indebtedness as the key to education and, hence, social mobility.[10]

Growing student movements across the world, particularly in the 2011
cycle of protests, have drawn attention to the exploitative processes at play
within the marketization of education. As anthropologist Cristian Cabalin
argues in resonance with what I discussed in chapter two, neoliberal capitalism has turned education into an investment market of crucial importance to financial networks.[11] In this scenario, neoliberal capitalism performs as a machine that transforms the right to education into the right to
receive credit.[12] Neoliberal reason—which is predicated on freedom of
choice, market rationality, and the production of the self—promotes credit
as an empowering tool tied to the project of self-fashioning of prospective
proprietors.[13] Nevertheless, the dark side of credit, debt, turns students
into precarious workers. Conditioned by indebtedness, students' relation
to knowledge becomes functional, and knowledge acquisition comes to be
increasingly understood as "intellectual availability to exploitation," as
Marxist theorist and activist Franco "Bifo" Berardi asserts.[14]

In countries where education is offered as a consumer good that requires borrowing money, debt becomes a disciplining mechanism, theorized by Stefano Harney and Fred Moten as "debt governance."[15] In the context discussed here, debt governance is facilitated by the government's redefinition of its role from a guarantor of universal access to education to a sponsor of the right to credit.[16] While the notion of education as a right is premised on the government's obligation to its citizens, the defunding and privatization of public education, and the consequent student population indebtedness, reframes the relation between the state and citizens as one between owners and nonowners of capital. Thus redefined, this relationship unfolds in time, structured around the promise of repayment.[17]

Students are subsequently cast as debtors within a form of parasite capitalism that, as Maurizio Lazzarato claims, deprives them of "political power, of the future, of time."[18] As a social relation between owners and nonowners of capital that unfolds in time, debt performs a crucial function in the production of subjectivity, a process that Lazzarato theorizes as "the making of the indebted man."[19] As a mode of subjectivation, indebtedness entails a structuring of vital time as time lived toward fulfilling debt obligations. That is why a crucial aspect of the students' protest performances is that they enabled students not only to appear as victims denouncing credit as financial vampirism but to enact a counterhegemonic positioning. Using performance as an enactment of sovereignty over their time (and bodies), students deployed a collective assertion of agency, delinking themselves from the creditor-debtor relation.

UNDOING DEBT TIME: THE "FEARLESS GENERATION"

Drawing inspiration from a previous cycle of high school student mobilization (the 2006 "Penguin Revolution") in 2011 university and high school students sustained seven months of collective action, from April to November.[20] The mobilized students combined traditional methods of social mobilization such as assemblies, occupations, strikes, and rallies (mainly coordinated through the governance of the CONFECH) with multiple decentralized protest performances.[21] In protest performances such as kiss-ins and flash mobs, students used stylized behavior tactically in order to circumvent police repression and counteract the negative media coverage that depicted their protests as violent and disruptive.[22] Students deployed positive emotions and dispositions such as love, communal organization, sacrifice, and resolve to legitimate and sustain their movement in a period of increased protest criminalization. The first generation to be born into democracy, students became increasingly identified as "the fearless generation." This name indicated that the students' life experiences radically differed from their parents' and grandparents' traumatic past under authoritarian rule.[23]

Writer Diamela Eltit, member of CADA, Colectivo de Acciones de Arte (Art Actions Collective), a group that was active during Pinochet's dictatorship, argues that the success of the student movement as a turning point after forty years of education reform demands was due to the students' use of multiple tactics. Eltit states that the movement's "subversive demand" to make education free was effectively sustained through "a system of assemblies, the logic of self-representation, aesthetics, bodies, image and space appropriation, mass media, tribal and indigenous issues, and sci-fi."[24]

Eltit's praise of the students' tactics is fitting since there are important resonances between CADA and the students' use of aesthetics as a tool for political intervention, despite the different contexts in which CADA and the students operated. The following statement by CADA's cultural critic Nelly Richard, characterizing the collective's intervention during Pinochet's dictatorship, illuminates the core of CADA's performative disruption of Pinochet's authoritarian order. Richard states that CADA intervened in

a context where it [was] essential to experiment with the transformation of reality, to rectify the real in order to make it intelligible or workable, to use the language of creativity to undermine the language of dominance, to de-authorize the meaning and repressive policies of that regime which . . . imposed on the individual and collective body the metaphors of terror and misery.[25]

Although the students' decentralized, expanded use of performance in 2011 radically differs from CADA's avant-garde artistic gestures under Pinochet's dictatorship, Richard's statement signals many aspects at play in the students' protest performances, such as intelligibility, delegitimation, and transformation. Both in CADA's artistic interventions and in the students' protest performances, the use of aesthetics has a performative function, that is, it serves as an expressive *and* transmuting response to official discourses that promote debt as investment, education as entrepreneurship, and citizenship as self-management. If, as the Argentine crisis of 2001 revealed, neoliberal states are founded on sovereign debt as a way of transforming industrial economies into financial havens of nomadic capital, their upgraded versions in the late 2000s function as bridges between capital and bodies so that "detachable" capital may "attach" to life prospects for profit. This is why embodied protest performances in physical and digital spaces are crucial modes of intervention to "undermine the language of dominance" and the micropolitical workings of neoliberal governance and governmentality.

Resonating with previous uses of the aesthetic as a key component of oppositional, subversive practices, in 2011 students articulated bodies, images, and new media in multiplatform performance constellations, crafting their demands in inventive ways to confront the hegemony of the neoliberal state, influence public opinion, and galvanize collective dissent. Social media played an instrumental role in the 2011 mobilization, enabling students to decentralize their elaborated choreographies by extending the eventness of their protest performances. Through digital networking, students maintained, and at the same time complicated, the experience of liveness and copresence that defines live art and theatrical performance in order to expand their social movement beyond tight networks of everyday activism. By both maintaining and complicating the experience of liveness and copresence, in street flash mobs and their online dissemination, students were able to expand their movement, implicating potential supporters corporeally to make their case for public education as a matter of national concern rather than self-interest.

DISTRIBUTED CHOREOGRAPHIES: FLASH MOB CONVERGENCE AND THE EXTENDED EVENT

july 7 Thriller FOR EDUCATION moves to Antofagasta

FINAL NOTICE

Tomorrow at noon, ALL SLUGGISH PEOPLE who didn't attend today's rehearsal have to be in the CLINIC AREA so that we can integrate them into one of the four blocks!

REMEMBER the part that goes before the dance, listen attentively, and remember the sounds that you should make:
"BRRRRRRRRRRRRRRRRRRRRRRRRRRRRR" hahahaha! = P

Costuming:

Everyone is responsible for their own costumes, make yourself the best zombie outfit that you can, be creative, WE WILL NOT DANCE in our uniforms or with school insignias.

Stick signs and stuff related to your death caused by the lack of education, the death of your dreams ETC. on your outfit.

Makeup:

It's personal and optional too; however, *we uploaded tutorials* on how to do your own makeup, and on Thursday we'll have people available to help those who have problems.

IT'S STRICTLY PROHIBITED to shout during the convergence and the dance performance the NAME OF YOUR SCHOOLS or ANY INTELLIGIBLE WORD OF ANY TYPE.

Zombies do not speak. They make the typical "groan."

Please *pass along the information through this medium.*

We'll coordinate rehearsals.

We have several colleagues who danced this in STGO [Santiago] and who are *motivated to repeat* it in honor of their four thousand peers who danced in front of LA MONEDA! :D

Let's get motivated!![26]

This is how the organizers of *Thriller por la educación* in the northern city of Antofagasta, performed twelve days after the Santiago version, addressed prospective participants on their Facebook event page. Social media in this case functioned as a catalyzer of social mobilization, as argued by Paolo Gerbaudo.[27] While laying out the rules and the aesthetics of the event (no school uniforms, zombies don't speak) the flash mob coordinator encouraged self-styling ("make yourself the best zombie outfit that you can") as an incentive for participation. This demonstrates that activists use social media not merely to coordinate details but to create the affective preconditions that are necessary to spark social mobilization, thus shaping the protest as a collective act that is enhanced by individual creativity.

The flash mob organizers' use of YouTube video tutorials further manifests the generative role of social media as an action-oriented tool beyond information dissemination. Through their movement and makeup video tutorials, the *Thriller* flash mob organizers not only transmitted preparatory materials; they also created the experience of asynchronic cooperation that animates performance constellations. In movement tutorials, organizers broke down *Thriller*'s choreography, creating sequences to be mirrored by those not able to join rehearsals. In contrast to these instructional videos that bridged classrooms or other shared spaces with prospective participants' homes, makeup tutorials show intimate spaces such as the organizers' bedrooms. In one of them, the instructor uses written signs to guide would-be zombies through the makeup process, disclosing the fact that she can't speak because her brother is sleeping.[28]

Through movement mirroring or through a webcam-induced sense of a face-to-face meeting, these videos contribute to sustaining the experience of shared collaboration that is crucial to catalyzing street mobilization in an era of information overload and social fragmentation.[29] These examples show how, through social media constructions of real-time, digitally mediated and bodily performance intertwine in cogenerative dynamics, making nonsimultaneous acts be felt as part of an extended event.

As media scholar Jason Farman argues, new technologies such as mobile communication devices redefine notions of spatiality and embodiment, altering the way we navigate offline environments.[30] As we experience daily in our interactions through applications such as WhatsApp, the digital is an integral component of our everyday life rather than a separate, optional realm. In an era of continual communication, digital audio messages, for example, are signals that interlocutors exchange with the presumption of an ongoing conversation and the sustained presence of addressees. These technological changes are crucial to creating the conditions of extended copresence and liveness that is part of an asynchronous performance constellation.[31] Thus, the question is not what media or activity is more crucial to protest mobilization, online or offline, but rather how social movements take advantage of our transmedia moment, a moment defined by a cross-pollination of multiple systems of communication.

In Chile, the students' articulation of media and spaces in asynchronic performance constellations that extend copresence beyond physical and temporal simultaneity is tactical. As in many regions of the world today, public space is regulated, especially in what concerns massive demonstrations. Rallies and marches require permits through which authorities control crowd movement or even hinder mass convergence altogether. During the Chilean student protests, as rallies and marches became more frequent and sustained, the government deployed this strategy effectively, managing street demonstrations in ways that diminished the force of students' acts of dissent, for example, reducing the duration of protests or banning students from access to vital city arteries. Thus, flash mobs and other creative protests facilitated by social media provided students with mechanisms that enabled them to dodge government control strategies and achieve a sustained attention effect while being economical with regards to time and space. Flash mobs in this case function as "soft," tactical modalities intertwining bodies and digitally networked mediation in order to tackle with "heavy," strategic, power structures enforced by the state and the police.

Thriller for Education is an example of creative activism in which collective acts such as occupations, rallies, or demonstrations are enhanced through aesthetic features that engage participants and spectators affectively.[32] Besides building on a tradition of citizens' occupation of public space to voice their demands, *Thriller for Education* drew from popular culture, zombie subculture, and viral culture. These influences provided the foundation for a particular kind of street protest that aligned with the carnivalesque, poetic style of 1990s protest movements such as the Zapatistas and the 1999 antiglobalization demonstrations in Seattle. As demonstrated by the event text quoted from Facebook, the participatory impetus of the performance was enhanced by social media practices that participate in derivative processes of circulation, appropriation, and change.

Flash mobs are hybrid performances organized, documented, and disseminated through mobile communication and social media platforms. "Swarming," or flash convergence, is facilitated by computational technologies that are part of an era of wireless, ubiquitous connectivity that danah boyd describes as the "always-on lifestyle."[33] The unpredictability of flash performance as an impromptu event, its unforeseen emergence in the urban landscape, strongly depends on the technologies implemented to ensure the replication and spreadability of learned gestures to potential reperformers. In this sense, what we see as a radical expression of embodied convergence in physical space is both informed and enabled by so-called disembodied technologies. Contemporary technologies of networked cooperation shape how bodies appear in street protests as such mediation becomes a crucial vehicle for self-assertion and collective action.

However, even though performance constellations question the primacy of the street event, upsetting the hierarchy that positions social media activism as merely complementary to street protests, physically grounded performances are the "what" of the transmedia protests, either literally as in flash mobs or figuratively as in virtual sit-ins as acts of kinesthetic imagination. In situ, collective action is what incited participants of the *Thriller* flash mob to rehearse and design their costumes, and it was what compelled supporters to join by "replaying" it on social media.

This means that there are cultural and historical resonances besides technological affordances that drive people to reactivate Jackson's choreography. As a body-to-body act of transfer that epitomizes the generative role of new media in contemporary performance, *Thriller* transmits more than a pop culture story. In the Chilean context, this choreography links the 2010s debt crisis to the 1980s US process of deindustrialization, and, in that sense, it creates an additional vector in a broader performance constellation that spans across borders, sparking insurgent moves against capitalist mutations.[34]

"IT'S CLOSE TO MIDNIGHT AND SOMETHING EVIL'S LURKING IN THE DARK": DANCING DEINDUSTRIALIZATION

Thriller's choreography was created by Michael Peters and Michael Jackson for the 1983 music video of the same title. As a hallmark of the emergence of the music video genre, *Thriller* bears an interesting relation to technological mediation, traveling from televisual representation to vernacular appropriation via digital circulation. Within the genre of flash mob performances, the *Thriller* choreography has become canonical as it has been reperformed by fans all over the world. Social media are central to this process of iteration of the choreography, offering a vernacular repository of *Thriller* flash mob performances. If in the 2000s cell phone communication facilitated the emergence of flash mobs, enabling leaderless coordination, in the 2010s social media contributed important features such as networked dissemination as an essential element in the visibility and aftereffects of swarming performances.

Performance studies scholar Judith Hamera argues that what drives fans to reperform *Thriller* is Jackson's seemingly effortless choreographic precision that she defines as "precarious excellence."[35] Grounding her analysis of the choreography in the context of Reagan's reengineering of the US economy, Hamera reads Jackson's precarious virtuosity as a representation of the shift from industrialization to the transnational modes of outsourced production that characterize neoliberal globalization. This is, in Hamera's view, another crucial factor of *Thriller* fans' drive to consume *and* replicate the choreography beyond the specificities of Jackson's technical work. Performing as the vanishing motor of the industrial era through what Hamera calls "percussive liquidity,"[36] Jackson became a generator of reperformances by those longing for the (not so humane either) lost phase of industrial production before capital and labor became deterritorialized or, as Zygmunt Bauman puts it, "liquified."[37]

The resurgence of undead bodies in Chile within a moment of diffused

Figure 5: "Morí debiendo" (I died owing). *Thriller por la educación*, zombie flash mob in Santiago de Chile, June 24, 2011. Photo courtesy of Diego Salinas Flores / Colectivo Fauna.

global, anticapitalist zombie protests can thus be understood as a post-Fordist Western Hemispheric dance that connects histories of deindustrialization to dramas of financialization. The percussive liquidity of Jackson's fragmented movement vocabulary allegorizing the death of industrialization is transformed in the Chilean context into the shattered movement of bodies crushed under the burden of indebtedness.

In the Chilean context, *Thriller for Education* dramatizes the (undead) life of flexible workers in permanent training as a source of capital investment and neoliberal gain.[38] Linking Jackson's 1980s and the Chilean students' 2010s as well as histories of both democratic and authoritarian implementations of neoliberal policies, *Thriller*'s performance constellation foregrounds broken movement as the effect of the mutations of neoliberal capitalism affecting workers and students in the Western Hemisphere.

Performance studies scholar Rebecca Schneider complicates readings of zombie marches as acts of collective agency within so called creative, affective capitalism.[39] Schneider analyzes the Occupy Wall Street zombie protests as depictions of Marx's notion of unused capital as dead capital and its reactivation through living labor. Schneider explains that, because capital necessitates circulation to produce accumulation, in deindustrialized societies "vampire-like" capital extracts surplus from living labor, that is, from liveness itself (or from "being alive*ness*") understood as labor. In light of this process, Schneider crucially asks if, by producing viral materials and thus participating in social media's content circulation, performances such as zombie marches undo or rather reanimate the machinery of capitalism "in a drama of parasitism."[40] This means that students are not only hosts of predatory lending but also willing surplus value producers for those profiting from free networked labor and data mining.[41]

This is a widespread concern that particularly occupies critics of social media as corporate platforms of immaterial capitalism. Despite this legitimate caveat, the tactical importance of these channels cannot be underestimated or rejected, particularly in contexts of media monopolization and protest repression, as I explained earlier. Even though they definitely contributed to what Jodi Dean calls "communicative capitalism," the Chilean students also appropriated these channels to successfully install (and delegitimize) the issue of generational indebtedness in the national agenda. I agree with Schneider that social media virality doubles the parasitism denounced in the performance, but this does not necessarily mean that the gesture of denunciation lost its potentially transformative force. If the students cannot avoid being hosts of capitalism in one way or another, their *Thriller* viral performance does not mean that they accept this uncritically but, rather, that that they employ it tactically, complementing other political interventions, including those centralized in student organizations.

UNDEAD PERFORMANCES:
LIVING IN THE AFTERLIFE OF THE EVENT

As we saw in the *Thriller for Education* Facebook post, social media interactions enable processes of asynchronic coordination that are key to sustain powerful, choreographed, seemingly impromptu events such as flash mobs. In the era of wireless connectivity and mobile communication, social media strengthens these hit-and-run incidents by extending them spatially and temporally through user-generated digital archives and viral circulation. As shown in a video of the flash mob performance in Santiago posted on YouTube on June 24, 2011, spectators watched the event through their cameras in an act that wove together live performance and mediated reproduction.[42] This is a clear sign of the hybrid presence of spectators in both physical and social media spaces, facilitated by "always on" mobile communication culture and by the breaking-news content economy of platforms such as Facebook and Twitter.[43]

Contemporary flash mob performances differ from their cell phone predecessors in that they are acts of convergence in physical space as well as events distributed by social media. They demonstrate that, in contemporary performance constellations, the boundaries between performance as original act and the document or memory of the act are more porous than when analog photography and video recording functioned as technologies of capture. Mobile media technologies of live documentation and transmission combine with the media-sharing economy, producing traces of the event that preserve its eventness to prompt further participation. Thus, even though the shared videos and photographs of street protests do not necessarily *change* the event (as contingent occurrences might transform a live performance) social media create a strong sense of belonging and ownership through which supporters expand—and sometimes complicate—social movements' self-narrative.

Performance's "only life" in the present of its execution is replaced in the digital era by performance's "many lives," when the documentation of a performance activates new iterations via digital archives.[44] Unlike traditional, analogic archives, digital archives do not merely document or register the event of performance attempting to arrest its ephemerality. As Diana Taylor claims, digital archives *"require,* rather than *resist,* the change over time."[45] This is because, as Wendy Hui Kyong Chun states, despite being considered a more efficient and durable system of storage than analog sources, digital media are, like performance, ephemeral repositories of memory that rely on repetition and process to fight obsolescence.[46] As the myriad of interactions surrounding *Thriller* demonstrate, user-generated content in social media platforms is not peripheral to the street event as something that *was*; social media replications enliven a performance, transforming it into an asynchronous performance constellation that builds on attention economies driven by "freshness" and content relevance as networked, asynchronous versions of liveness.

Social media redefine liveness as "live feed," a digital paradigm predicated on the assumption of the continuous presence of interlocutors. As Philip Auslander argues, liveness can no longer be defined exclusively by the copresence of performers and spectators.[47] In the digital era, liveness is constituted by people's affective responses to technological demands such as Facebook's "What's on your mind?" or Twitter's "It's what's happening," which create the sense of immediacy that we experience as "real-time."[48] Within the always-on lifestyle engineered by wireless connectivity, "being present" means both sharing the here and now of an event and enacting its reiteration online via instant reporting, live streaming, and digital documentation.

In the Chilean students' *Thriller* flash mob, as I explained, this contributed to expanding a tactically short event into a distributed choreography, a performance constellation of extended eventness. In the case of our next example, social media mobilization maintained the intensity of a durational on-the-ground happening, entangling disjointed spaces and temporalities of participation. The durational specificity of this street performance opened opportunities not only for participants to engage with the city and quotidian time in nonconventional ways; it also allowed the emergence of spaces of deliberation where citizens discussed the future of education and its relation to the country's development. This was another contribution from the "fearless generation" to an intergenerational discussion that sought to upset the hegemony of debt governance and debt time.

RUNNING TIME:
CIRCULAR TACTICS AND EXPANDED BELONGING

The frame shows a blackout image accompanied by the sound of a beating heart. A phrase appears in three consecutive inserts: "1800 / horas / por una educación gratuita" (1,800 / hours / for free education). Next, we see several close-up shots featuring a series of sneakers and legs performing warm-up movements. Uplifting music starts and a traveling shot follows a group of runners of various ages traversing an urban landscape. One of the runners carries a small Chilean flag; another, a black flag with white letters reading "Educación Gratuita Ahora" (Free Education Now). New words are superimposed on the image: "Más de 3000 corredores / La bandera de la educación ha dado más de 8800 vueltas / 50 días de trote contínuo / 8 minutos toma una vuelta promedio" (More than 3,000 runners / The education flag has given 8,800 rounds / 50 days of uninterrupted running / Each round takes 8 minutes in average). Toward the end of this video, the music recedes and the heartbeat sound is audible again. On a black background a text addresses viewers directly: "Sólo 8 minutos de tu vida. Ven a correr" (It only takes 8 minutes of your life. Come run with us).

With this video by Edison Cájas uploaded on Vimeo on Saturday, August 7, 2011, at 9:11 p.m., those involved in the durational performance *1,800 Hours for Education* engaged viewers as potential participants.[49] With twenty-five days more to go until the closing line, runners were on demand.

Even though this video does not have an instructional function like the *Thriller for Education* tutorials, it seeks to incite social media users to join the street protest and become part of the movement by literally moving with activists and organizers.

1,800 Hours for Education, a durational protest performance launched on June 13, 2011, was conceived by students of the drama school of the Universidad de Chile during an assembly when they discussed alternatives to the massive protests that the government and the media demonized. Building on a suggestion by one of the assembly's attendees who proposed running around the government house (La Moneda) for a day, Sergio Gilabert, a twenty-three-year-old drama student, suggested escalating the challenge by significantly extending the run to cover eighteen hundred continuous hours.[50] This number symbolized the amount of money needed to cover one year of college tuition. If *Thriller* tackled with the long-term effects of cumulative debt via flash convergence, *1,800 Hours* followed the opposite principle, aiming to put an end to indefinite indebtedness by engaging bodies in sustained, collective effort.

As soon as they launched the project and started to run, students created a Facebook page to invite participants to join. The first Facebook post, dated June 13, jump-starts the project, depicting demonstrators as heroes determined to save public education. The post features a flyer that contains a Batman-like figure running by a coin. It uses a messianic approach in order to move prospective participants to contribute their individual physical effort toward a collective goal: "Run! 1,800 Hours for Education. Around the government house from June 13 to August 26. I move for free education! Come and join!"[51]

In *1,800 Hours*, participants took turns encircling the government house in Santiago during two and a half months, day and night and under winter weather conditions. The run can be read as the ambulatory version of the tactic of occupying or blocking access to a building by "embracing" it. The image of the embrace communicates a nonviolent version of more confrontational tactics such as blockade and occupation. As a mobile occupation of space, *1,800 Hours* involved the use of a circular, insistent mode of corporeal engagement with a historically charged space, La Moneda, a building that evokes traumatic events such as the violent ousting of socialist president Salvador Allende by Pinochet in the 1973 coup d'état.

Because of its durational character *1,800 Hours* necessitated a strong digital component that would help sustain the performance's required effort and momentum. The *1,800 Hours* Facebook page, the @1800Horas Twitter account, and promotional videos such as Cajas's helped create a

Figure 6: *1800 horas por la educación*, durational protest performance, Santiago de Chile, June 13–August 27, 2011. Photo courtesy of Diego Salinas Flores / Colectivo Fauna.

feedback loop between the event in physical space and its social media presence. Through this feedback loop social media affordances contributed visibility and also prospective performers: organizers recruited runners and supporters, announcing on the event's pages the goals achieved within the proposed duration of the run.[52] Through social media engagement organizers disrupted the clear-cut distinction between performers and witnesses that characterizes artistic performances by addressing social media users as coparticipants.

From a symbolic standpoint, the cumulative number of hours of physical effort that participants dedicated toward a future of free education functioned as the counterpoint image to the growing numbers of debt accumulated by students and their families. Following the rising negative appraisal of the status of education in Chile, individual debt numbers started surfacing as part of a general sentiment of disidentification with the narrative of self-sufficiency and investment promoted by the neoliberal government. Projects such as http//:www.YoDebo.cl, a website launched on June 6, 2011, by a group of engineering students of Universidad de Chile, an institution formerly fully funded by the state, offered a platform for protesters to add a face to debt numbers and to narrate a different version of the government's story. The website produced a collective number that crystallized what most people were otherwise not able to fathom.

Similar to YoDebo.cl, *1,800 Hours* socialized individual burden and transformed individual vulnerability into the basis for sustainable effort. By inviting participants to join a protest that could only be sustained through a collective effort distributed over the course of seventy-five days, in *1,800 Hours* students countered the logic of personal responsibility and the effects of cumulative debt on individual bodies. The ethos of "sharing debt" was accompanied by a socialization of the labor of performance.

Decentralizing the experience, that is, sharing responsibility for the development of the performance with participants outside the circle of drama students, was important pragmatically and ideologically: pragmatically because students needed many bodies to sustain the protest over its intended duration; ideologically because it reflected in the actual practice of the protest the students' framing of their struggle as part of broader misgivings about the effects of neoliberal policies in Chilean society.

This ethos of inclusion turned the eighteen-hundred-hour run into a political event configured not merely as a form of public address but as a movement characterized by what Alain Badiou defines as a "belonging to all."[53] We see this in the cover picture of the *1,800 Hours* Facebook page, which includes an image of a boy carrying a Chilean flag overlaid with the legend "Thank you."[54]

The run's social media presence not only catalyzed but also helped sustain the force of the offline event. Even though, in a strict sense, the Facebook fan page is less interactive than a virtual sit-in or an online cacerolazo, both of which sought to create an engaging experience for participants, the *1,800 Hours* online components played a key role in generating opportunities for participants to join the event and sustain its eventness. Through updates, calls for runners, milestone reports, and posts containing documentary materials, a boundary-defying happening that was difficult to encompass given its duration was enlivened and multiplied.[55] This was an overall goal that informed the use of performance in the 2011 student protests cycle. Resorting to technological innovation and creativity, the students not only updated protest methods to their generation's preferences but also sought to fight the demoralization and exhaustion that plague processes of sustained, direct democracy.[56]

Whether or not social media culture informed the students' action in an explicit way beyond its communicative function, social media dynamics did perfectly match the drive to distribute responsibility for an ambitious collective endeavor as widely as possible. Even those who were not able or willing to run had their place in the performance. This was manifested most notably in what students called "the installation," a makeshift kiosk with contributions to support runners such as food and clothes. "The installation" provided a stationary option for those who were compelled by the *1,800 Hours* run, and it became a site of assembly where people discussed ongoing events that were part of the city's mobilized everydayness during that time.[57] The sustained synchronous and asynchronous modes of shared effort required by the laborious specificity of this action created conditions for collective belonging and radical democracy to emerge. Thus, *1,800 Hours for Education* demonstrates the significance of tactical uses of performance as an open happening enacting the disruption of both the status quo and futurity in the present. In *1,800 Hours* protesters put in motion temporalities alternative to debt time by choreographing contiguous and noncontiguous relations into collective action.

AT THE FINISH LINE: WHAT MOVES YOU

As documented in the run's daily notebook, by the end of the eighteen hundred hours, five thousand people had participated in the marathon.[58] The narrative of a shared effort and determination that was central to *1,800 Hours* as a tactical intervention was developed and advanced by the constellative dramaturgy facilitated by social media communication networks. This enabled the public to not only watch what they were not able to experience directly given the long duration of the event, but also to become what Zizi Papacharissi calls "affective publics."[59] Through the dynamic created between people, technology, and social practices, social media users became attuned to a collective expression of resolve that sought to prompt the state to redefine its approach to education, at a moment when representatives and state officials discussed who should pay for education.

Contesting the performativity of the promise of debt repayment as an effect of debt governance on indebted bodies, social media provided a tool to undergird the project of using bodily expenditure to spur social transformation. Social media also provided students and supporters with a platform to frame the action in their own terms. Whereas mass media usually depict protesters as disruptive of the city's capital flow, social media facilitate collaborative coverage, that is, bottom-up, decentered, autonomous, and redundant information.[60] Such a collaborative effort draws its power from the ability to produce a news agenda that would otherwise escape the attention of the mass media.[61]

However, in spite of its success in enticing supporters to join or to follow the durational performance, at the end of *1,800 Hours* the money to cover tuition for the students enrolled in public universities obviously did not materialize. Nevertheless, the protest was not perceived as a failure because from the start, the terms in which it was built defied categories of success, and it was perhaps even meant to foreground contrasting feelings. In a personal interview, Gilabert stated that even though the protest was not successful, it was necessary: it showed that students had a deep commitment to improve their and their families' circumstances, and it enabled five thousand people to come together to manifest and support the movement's goals.

As a drama student, Gilabert emphasized the corporeal aspect of the protest as an ethical stance. He asked: "How do you want me to tell you [we want public education]? Dancing? Playing zombie? Running?"[62] And, yet, still nothing . . . The online newspaper *Clinic Online* registers this paradoxical aspect of *1,800 Hours'* tactical use of failure in an article titled: "In 1,800 Hours the Government Didn't Move for Education."[63] Mobilizing what at the time seemed like an ambitious ideal (free, public, and high-quality education) through a seemingly impossible goal (the eighteen-hundred-hour run), Chilean students and their supporters were able to put "nonperformers" on the spot and confront the government through a symbolic action that foregrounded concrete steps toward solving the problem. If protesters were able to contribute their collective effort toward achieving a seemingly impossible goal, why wouldn't the government do its part?

As an iterative and aggregative performance that took the issue of education out of the frame of personal investment and debt as common sense, *1,800 Hours* sought to symbolically propel participants into a future of free education. If the debt economy entails a process of subjectivation that creates in bodies a memory of accountability for the future (that is, of being accountable to the promise of debt repayment), using performance and digital networking as iterative behavior, participants in the eighteen-hundred-hour marathon created another kind of embodied, collective memory. Through performance as an open, contingent event, runners and supporters contested finance's neutralization of time and political power, distributing engaged action across nonlinear and recursive temporalities through which they emerged to themselves and Chilean society as legitimate political actors.

BECOMING OTHERWISE

To counteract the effects of a debt economy invested in "making man uniform, predictable, orderly,"[64] Chilean students mobilized contrasting ways
of occupying public space that were enhanced, sustained, and multiplied
by asynchronic modes of cooperation supported by digital platforms.
Through their transmedia protest performances, students materialized
notions of radical democracy that transformed indebted subjects into mobilized social actors. Working through various temporalities, platforms, and
agents (allegorical figures such as zombies and messianic marathon runners), the student movement revealed the problematic foundations of the
neoliberal state and its transformation of education from a social investment into a burdensome consumer good. Through performative protests,
Chilean students experimented with forms of embodiment and digital
coordination, circulation, and eventness that functioned as tactics for "making sensible"[65] (and disentangling from) the effects of a system that profits
from human capital and vulnerability. By choreographing collective action
on- and offline, students provided platforms for citizens to reclaim education as a right and thus redefine their relationship to the state.

Through social networking, students were able to accrue critical mass
and accelerate coordination and resource mobilization. Digital tools,
mainly blogs and photologs, had already been a strong component within
the 2006 high school students' protests. However, whereas the platforms
that were popular in 2006 involved a one-to-many mode of communication, the tools of choice in 2011, Facebook and Twitter, facilitated a many-
to-many mode of communication. This enabled activists to expand their
movement, implicating sectors that had been apathetic or fearful to express
political dissent in the past. Through these decentralized, distributed performances, activists garnered widening support in their debunking of the
rhetoric of privatized education that fostered personal investment as a key
to successful individual futures. The entanglement between synchronous
and asynchronous collaboration across platforms facilitated modes of collective emergence that are crucial to counteract debt governance as an
extended and disempowering relation between debtors and creditors
within financial capitalism.

Foregrounding relations of convergence in physical space (flash mobs)
and online dispersion (viral sharing), the protest performances analyzed
here appropriated late capital's dynamics such as post-Fordist production
fragmentation and financial capital's openness to contingency for the pur-
pose of revitalizing democracy. By assembling bodily enactments in asyn-

chronous performance constellations, students articulated contrasting modes of temporality that challenged the hegemony of debt time. The forms of "againness" that were initiated iteratively across platforms and contexts functioned as ways of interrupting the timing of debt as the assertion of guilt pending full repayment. To permanence, they introduced discontinuity; to being (in debt), they offered "becoming otherwise"; to a "walking dead" existence, they offered epic runners bringing forth livable futures in the present.

FOUR

Contesting Disappearance
after Ayotzinapa

State Terror, Hashtags, and the
Pulsating Event

As those who participate in contemporary protests know, hashtags are
key tools for social mobilization. Hashtags are keywords preceded by the
hash or numeral sign (#) used to contextualize a social media post or to
place it within a broader conversation. Because of their role as markers
and conductors of meaning and affect, hashtags have transcended their
function and social media locus, influencing a cultural shift in communication and politics. Linguist Michele Zappavigna describes this cultural
shift as "affiliation via findability" because, through hashtags, users can
track people's responses or direct reporting of critical events. As Zappavigna shows, hashtags foster particular modalities of community-
building that she describes as "ambient affiliation," manifested in the
formula "Search for me and affiliate with my values," which reveals the
paradoxical workings of social media as simultaneously self-centered
and communitarian platforms.[1]

The logic of affiliation lies at the very foundation of hashtags. In a 2007
tweet, technology expert Chris Messina submitted hashtags to users' consideration, proposing they be used to link tweets and thus group people
around common interests or topics. The hash, or "pound," sign as it is
known in the United States, had been already in use by Internet Relay Chat
communities to identify channels and topics.[2] Initially rejected by Twitter
executives as a "nerdy idea," hashtags were officially adopted in 2009 after
their central role during the San Diego forest fires.[3] A sign that had been
employed in telecommunication to terminate transmission was thus
revamped, consolidating Twitter as a networking, cooperative platform.[4]

As indexical and affiliative points of convergence, hashtags help users
search, retrieve, and disseminate news and commentary generated in Twitter's fast-paced, information-laden environment. Yarimar Bonilla and Jona-

than Rosa add a performative dimension to the functional uses of hashtags, stating that through them users indicate "a meaning that might not be otherwise apparent" in their posts.[5] Focusing on #Ferguson as a paradigmatic example, these authors show how the hashtag enabled activists to produce searchable information—aggregating responses to the murder of Mike Brown in Ferguson, Missouri—*and* to situate this case as part of antiblack institutional violence.[6] In this sense, hashtags such as #Ferguson are performative because they document episodes of police brutality and generate new forms of sociality that rework the materiality of black lives, contesting media depictions of African American men as "bad victims."[7]

Social media theorist José Van Dijck takes the idea of hashtags as taxonomic and performative tools a step farther, showing the centrality of these hyperlinked labels to Twitter's affective economy, particularly with regards to the category of "trending topics." Launched in late 2008, trending topics refer to the list that appears on users' home pages and on Twitter's main page showing the most popular hashtags at a global or national scale. As we will see later, trending topics are determined through an algorithm that captures intensity over relevance. That is, trending hashtags are not the most used but those that are more rapidly replicated. This variable puts influencers, that is, users who have a massive number of followers, in a better position than activists to trend, a fact that has deep implications for understanding the multiple forces that drive networked movements.

The trajectory of scholarly conceptualizations of the cultural and political significance of hashtags that I am tracing here thus moves from an organizational function (hashtags as indexical markers) to a semiotic and potentially more political function (hashtags as commentary), to an affective, interpellative mode ("Search for me and affiliate with my values *now!*") This trajectory suggests a displacement from a focus on the spatial organization or management of information to a more temporally driven focus on users' responses. This is due to the fact that Twitter enables users to post from their mobile phones, mimicking text messages, thus becoming the real-time social media platform par excellence and a key resource in framing an incident as a disruptive, political event.

In the field of social mobilization, tweets and hashtags allow activists to bring urgent issues into public awareness, put pressure on decision-makers, coordinate collective action, and build transnational alliances. Movements such as #BlackLivesMatter and #NiUnaMenos have recently shown that these social media forms effectively galvanize indignation into collective action, turning ambient affiliation into sustained participation.[8] Fashioning textual statements into affective vehicles of collective emotions, activists and social media users seek to influence public opinion and subjective change as preconditions to cultural, social, and political transformation. We see this in campaigns such as #IfTheyGunnedMeDown or #VivasNos-Queremos (#WeWantOurselvesAlive) that draw attention to the vulnerability of racialized and gendered bodies in contexts of deeply ingrained white supremacy and machismo. Moreover, used in tandem with "mentions" or direct addresses (Twitter's @ function), hashtags forge connections that extend or strategically supplement the necessary ties that constitute successful activism.[9]

While the force of twenty-first-century insurgent social movements cannot be attributed exclusively to hashtag use, a close analysis of the workings and function of these social media artifacts is critical to tracking the pacing of collective action, its articulation beyond specific contexts, and the new modalities of control that aim to limit their effects. To close our journey into the development of the entanglement between performance and digital networking within social protests and activisms in Latin America, here we will explore the role of hashtags as contested tools of resistance and control. Focusing on the case of the 2014 forced disappearance of forty-three students of a rural teachers' college in Ayotzinapa, Mexico, we will investigate how activists and protesters employed hashtags to counteract the government's demobilization strategies. The social media campaigns carried out in response to the students' abduction demonstrate how digitally networked practices usually associated with short-term, rapid-fire reaction such as hashtags and trending topics also enable more sustained protest events that I call pulsating performance constellations.

Rather than a feature that represents social media activism's short-term impact, as its critics claim, the instability of hashtags—what I call their *(a) liveness* within a sort of digital rhythm of generation, degeneration, and regeneration—is instrumental to sustain the momentum of networked protests and social movements. This is because social media's "what's happening" logic challenges activists to be "always on the move." As I explained in chapter 1, this approach was foregrounded by tactical media practitioners in the 1990s as a method to counteract the strategies of hegemonic powers designed to prevent, co-opt, or block contestation. In the 2010s, hashtag tactics not only include emergent responses to deterrent strategies; they also involve the recuperation of undead, previously circulated hashtags, reinvigorating them with new life as activists add new dimensions to their sustained and entangled struggles. In this sense, hashtags enable activists to aggregate responses, foster affiliation, and accumulate affective intensity, generating conditions to precipitate subjective and social change.

Precisely because hashtags are part of a system of real-time, immediate, gut responses as well as sustained mobilization, their temporal and affective dynamics are important resources to fight hegemonic strategies that aim to dissipate civic engagement back into smooth consensus and apathy. Hashtags combine the ephemerality of performance (a system propelled by embodied repetition) and the "enduring ephemerality" of digital media (a system of memory/preservation characterized by processes of degeneration and regeneration such as algorithmic indexing and filtering). Thus, the pulsating performance constellations that hashtags enable in their temporal and affective unfolding manifest the crucial intertwinement between symbolic, embodied performance, and digitally mediated performativity within contemporary activisms.

Here I will show how, besides their role in galvanizing protest events by aggregating responses to a critical event, hashtags perform as the units or *beats* of sustained campaigns or pulsating performance constellations. If, as we saw in chapter 3, choreographed performance and social media sharing allow activists to extend the heightened participatory appeal of protests beyond moments of spatial and temporal convergence, hashtags in turn mark the *tempo* or pace of networked protests, crystalizing moments of emergence, decline, and resurgence. As units of pulsating performance constellations, hashtags not only connect protesters across the various moments of a protest cycle; they also connect movements across borders, helping protesters highlight the systemic roots of social conflicts and bring historical perspective to breaking news events.

Thus, hashtags redefine participants' real-time protest experiences into a pulsating form of liveness, linking emergence and ephemerality to memory and historicity. This is a digitally mediated phenomenon that updates what live art theorist Adrian Heathfield calls performance's "varied deployments of altered time," that is, the fact that the *being there* of performance is always complicated by a connection with the past and the proximate future of its evanescence.[10] Through pulsating performance constellations, digital activists in Mexico challenged the government's repression of collective dissent, and they gave a transnational dimension to their movement, connecting the Ayotzinapa incidents to institutional violence north of their border. This northbound connection was also significant because of the role played by the United States concerning the Ayotzinapa case, such as the War on Drugs and practices of transnational resource extraction.

To understand how activists use hashtags configuring performance constellations that articulate temporality and affective intensity, let us turn to the 2014 political situation in Mexico, the context in which the Ayotzinapa case appeared as a turning point that disrupted the normalization of violence. This scenario presents a new entanglement between state violence and neoliberalism, this time accompanied by narco violence.

#SAVINGMEXICO-#SLAYINGMEXICO:
BREAKING CONSENSUS THROUGH NETWORKED PARODY

February 24, 2014. In the midst of the so-called Mexican moment, a period of structural political and economic changes such as the privatization of national oil reserves, Mexican president Enrique Peña Nieto makes the cover of *Time* magazine. Peña Nieto's businesslike, confident image is framed by a headline that evokes the Spanish colonizers' evangelical era: "Saving Mexico." However, this time, the redeeming mission does not involve delivering the word of God to "the barbarians" but implementing "sweeping reforms," (eleven to be more precise), in sectors such as energy, education, labor, finance, and telecommunications, approved by Congress in less than two years. The author of the magazine article that features Peña Nieto, Michael Crowley, argues that these reforms demonstrate the government's focus change "from the cartels to Mexico's economic potential."[11] Although Crowley's piece is not celebratory but rather critical of Peña Nieto's strategy of downplaying the problem of narco violence to attract foreign investment, the magazine cover triggers immediate reactions from outraged social media users. Similar to the way in which in 2001 Argentinians evaluated the government's performance, declaring "Out with them all," in 2014 Mexican protesters reacted to Peña Nieto's strategy by circulating memes, or parodic versions of the *Time* cover, tagged with the label #SavingMexico.[12] In contrast to Peña Nieto's pristine image, protesters' memes depict him as the embodiment of corporate greed or in military regalia, thus highlighting the state's violent management of rising popular discontent.

Contributing their own responses to the magazine cover, social media users transformed a static, mainstream media image into an evolving event. Twitter's algorithmic reward of intensity, turning widely and rapidly disseminated hashtags into trending topics, built on and choreographed indignation.[13] As the rapid-fire responses to the *Time* cover proliferated, the polemic "Saving Mexico" headline was transformed into the less ambiguous headline and hashtag, "Slaying Mexico." A hashtag that

Six-Year High Schools   Africa's Unholy War

TIME

SLAYING
MEXICO

HOW ENRIQUE PEÑA NIETO'S ... EPING REFORMS HAVE
CHANGED THE NARRATIVE IN ... ARCO-STAINED NATION

Figure 7: A meme depicting Peña Nieto as the Grim Reaper to condemn the effects of his policies.

could potentially be used as a mere reference to the magazine cover (#SavingMexico) became a commentary on the deadly orientation and effects of Peña Nieto's policies.[14]

In a context of increased militarization, censorship, and protest criminalization, social networks provided a platform for the emergence of a public sphere in which social media users denounced the government's accountability in Mexico's critical situation. Networked protesters not only reversed "Saving Mexico" into the ironic #SavingMexico. They also created a linear sequence, complementing "Saving Mexico" with "Slaying Mexico," thus linking the state's business-oriented activities to the violence that plagues the country, a connection that Peña Nieto's pristine image would render unimaginable to most readers of *Time*. As we saw in chapter 1, the elimination of workers' rights and land rights that followed the implementation of neoliberal reforms in the 1990s has required state and private violence to contain the rising popular resistance.[15] Through the memetic "Slaying Mexico" headline, protesters disrupted the normalization of violence and economic pillage with their own depiction of the "Mexican moment."

Using parody as a tactic of resistance, protesters appropriated what they saw as a cultural artifact directed to the English-speaking world of investors, skillfully inserting their voices within the social media environment as they had done less than two years before through the #YoSoy132 movement. In the Mexican context, this was a crucial tactical move rather than a slacktivist approach because social media are today an important space of contention. As activist and network analyst Erin Gallagher and others have demonstrated, in his 2012 presidential campaign and throughout his administration, in response to effective oppositional online mobilization Peña Nieto relied extensively on social media resources such as trolls and bots to fabricate support for his ambitious neoliberal reforms.[16]

Hashtag uses such as those exemplified by the #SavingMexico, #SlayingMexico series update tactics of *détournement*, also known as "culture jamming," that overturn or "derail" the intended message of a media artifact (for example, an image or text within a publicity) by modifying its main elements.[17] Thus, the targeted media artifacts are made to communicate their own critique, such as in the example of framing a proud and confident Peña Nieto with the sentence "Slaying Mexico." In this sense, parodic hashtags function as the Electronic Disturbance Theater's 404 File Not Found performances that made computer servers "confess" institutional abuse.

In their particular workings as time-based networked *détournements*, the #SavingMexico/#SlayingMexico hashtags and memes mark the high point of a pulsating performance constellation that subsequently drops and disappears from real-time social media experience as these hashtags lose their relevance or "freshness" in connection with a media event. The "gut responses" to the "Saving Mexico" *Time* cover will later turn into a more sustained engagement with the current state of Mexican democracy, a new cycle of social media-driven protest. Through hashtags as anchors of on- and offline pulsating performance constellations, activists developed tactics of persistence, contesting the government's strategies of dissipation and curtailment of popular unrest, and maintaining moments of intensity that accumulated in the development of an insurgent Mexican moment.

FROM #SAVINGMEXICO TO #WEAREALLAYOTZINAPA: SUSTAINING MOBILIZATION BEYOND HASHTAG INTENSITY

September 26, 2014. Seven months after the #SavingMexico-#SlayingMexico incidents triggered by the *Time* cover, one hundred students from the Ayotzinapa Rural Teachers' College are ambushed by police as they pass through the city of Iguala, in the Pacific Coast state of Guerrero, on their way to Mexico City to garner support for their school. During the ambush, three students are killed and forty-three detained and abducted. The government and mainstream media link the incident to Los Guerreros Unidos, a local criminal organization. The students, prospective rural teachers from an educational system and region known for cultivating community leaders, are cast as agitators who hijacked buses on their way to commemorate the anniversary of the 1968 student massacre of Tlatelolco.[18]

Enraged with the government's response to the forced disappearance of the forty-three students, Mexican activists organized massive demonstrations locally and around the world. These complemented assemblies, picket lines, and caravans led by relatives and friends of the Ayotzinapa students and supported by unions, students, and artists. Using the hashtags #Ayotzinapa or #TodosSomosAyotzinapa (#WeAreAllAyotzinapa), protesters converged online and offline to show solidarity with the students' families and the Mexican people. The students' black-and-white pictures, disseminated on social media captioned with the phrase "Vivos se los llevaron, vivos los queremos" (They were taken alive, we want them back alive), evoked the ID pictures of the disappeared carried by the Mothers of Plaza de Mayo in their rounds, as well as the Mothers' ongoing demand, "Aparición con vida" (We want them alive).

This connection reveals both the persistence of strategies of state violence even within democratic regimes as well as the persistence of legacies of a hemispheric history of activism contesting disappearance.[19] The ID pictures of the Ayotzinapa students stood in contrast with the images disseminated by mainstream media, which focused on the murdered students and treated victims as anonymous, statistical matter, thus reinforcing the students' erasure.[20]

The online mobilization for the Ayotzinapa students was complemented by offline installations displaying their pictures on school chairs. These installations transformed absence into a strong interpellation of Mexican and international authorities, and of publics made to bear witness to the students' forced disappearance. Throughout the world, particularly in educational institutions, supporters of the Mexican movement surrounding the Ayotzinapa case rejected a new episode of what Rossana Reguillo calls the "narco-machine,"[21] activating the students' still, bidimensional presence through a collective roll call that concluded with the word *Presente!*[22]

As the involvement of regional authorities in the forced disappearance of the students became clearer, dissident channels of communication

Figure 8: Ayotzinapa teach-in at New York University, December 10, 2014.
Photo courtesy of Lorie Novak.

proved crucial. Through street protest signs and hashtags such as #FueElEstado (#ItWasTheState) Mexican protesters put an end to the acceptance of the state's justification of victims' fate as "collateral damage" of the War on Drugs.[23] Besides rapid-fire, short-lived reactions to official declarations epitomized by trending hashtags, phrases such as "Quisieron enterrarnos, pero no sabían que éramos semilla" (They tried to bury us, but they didn't know we were seeds), discussed in the introduction, became widely circulated statements. They generated a sustained response to the government's attempts to diffuse public attention and bury the case.

This phrase became particularly poignant at a moment in which, in their search for the missing students, investigators discovered mass graves daily. "They tried to bury us, but they didn't know we were seeds" enacted a reversal procedure, similar to the "Saving Mexico" parodic appropriation. It reclaimed the meaning of "burial" from its entanglement with narco-machinic protocols, instead associating it with sowing, potentiality, immanence, and growth, meanings that evoke the world of the Ayotzinapa students as both rural teachers and defenders of education and land rights. In our predominantly visual culture, this phrase provided a poignant image that crystallized the contrast between the state's strategy of resorting to the figure of the disappeared to extinguish dissent, and the popular commitment to sustained mobilization that transformed the Ayotzinapa incident into the kernel of social transformation.

The street protests and the discursive and social media practices enacted by protesters in response to the disappearance of the *normalistas* of Ayotzinapa demonstrate the central role of networked symbolic action in the era of global connectivity and transnational governance. Forms of ritualized memorialization such as assembling forty-three chairs with the pictures of the missing students provided a template for activists and sympathizers to replicate the demand for justice in multiple sites around the world. The specter of human rights' violations perpetrated by the military and ruling elites in the Americas forced Mexicans to come face-to-face with the long-standing yet updated practices of state violence within a democratic, neoliberal regime. The forced disappearance of the *normalistas* incited a search for truth and a collective cry similar to the 1994's Zapatista "Ya basta!" (Enough is enough).[24]

Scholars such as Reguillo and Silvia Tabachnik share my conceptualization of networked movements as constitutive of disruptive, transformative events. Drawing on Badiou, Reguillo defines the "event" as a happening that exceeds a situation as we know it, in this case, an understanding of victims of violence as "collateral damage." According to Reguillo, the event that emerges through the doings of what she calls "insurrectionary subjectivities" helps us visualize what has been transformed; it materializes a new imaginary of human rights, of the right to protest, and of the true meaning of democracy. By repudiating official narratives, networked insurgencies "disorganize and uproot dominant power."[25] Building on the 2012 #YoSoy132 student movement, networked responses to #Ayotzinapa fleshed out connective mechanisms through which insurrectionary subjects contested the government's management of public opinion.

In turn, Tabachnik, drawing on Foucault, presents networked activisms in response to Ayotzinapa as strategic interventions that changed force relations, introducing questions ("What is happening to us?") that create fissures in media-motorized consensus. While hegemonic mass media aim to deactivate the force of an incident, framing it through "common sense" narratives, networked activists "name [the event], call it into being and actualize it in a multiplicity of devices."[26]

As these scholars note, events are never bounded; they are the result of events that precede them and are, in turn, the foundation of becomings that will follow them. My notion of performance constellations configuring a pulsating event visualizes the paradoxical, focused and also diffused, intensity of emerging happenings by anchoring key points in their development through an analysis of incipient and recuperated hashtags.

EMERGENCE AND MEMORY:
HASHTAGS AS PULSATING EPHEMERALS

As I explained earlier, hashtags are metadata tags or hyperlinked labels preceded by the number sign. Hashtags have become paradigmatic of how we process information. As media theorist Jeff Scheible claims, hashtags epitomize contemporary textual practices characterized by brevity and expression.[27] In this sense, hashtags and their usual hosts, tweets, are crucial communication tools for activists to generate ad hoc publics and underscore the significance of an issue. They are also integral to the way political leaders stage their presence in the public sphere, addressing their audiences, their opponents, and the media. Tweets indexed or nuanced by hashtags become ready-made, visually compelling sound bites for mass-media replication, used to give texture to news coverage. Hashtags are also important anchors to trace historical narrative.[28] They epitomize significant changes in the way electoral, partisan politics are managed today, with leaders having permanent direct contact with their constituents as well as being able to influence mainstream media agendas and public opinion in what we might call "populism 2.0."[29]

Hashtags are essential components of *technopolitics*, a contemporary form of political mobilization that appropriates or invents digital tools to generate collective action and organization.[30] As technopolitical tools, hashtags perform multiple functions: they focus social media users' attention on specific issues (#FreeChelseaManning) or help shape movements' identities (#BlackLivesMatter, #NiUnaMenos).[31] Hashtags install a sense of urgency (#NoWallNoBan), or help launch debates over ingrained cultural attitudes that severely compromise the lives of gendered and racially marked bodies (#NotAllMen- #YesAllWomen), looping back into street protests to address conditions of structural violence (#HandsUpDontShoot). Like graffiti, hashtags are gestured text, transmitting affect, argumentation, belonging, and dissensus. They provide the interpretive frame through which users engage with emergent issues. As Bonilla and Rosa claim, hashtags transform "posting about" into "participating in" a discussion or campaign.[32]

Besides their indexing and aggregating function, which can be seen as "spatial practices," hashtags perform along a temporal axis. Hashtags' pulsating rhythm is manifested when activists and protesters create, recycle, and resurface networked keywords, using them as vehicles of emergence, memory, and resurgence in order to sustain mobilization and to broaden the scope of specific claims.

Accordingly, hashtags manifest what Wendy Hui Kyong Chun calls "enduring ephemerality." With this concept, Chun draws attention to the fact that digital memory, usually conceived as a means of long-lasting preservation, is in fact defined by features such as malleability and modularity that draw digital memory closer to embodied memory processes than to "traditional" forms of archival arrest.[33] Processes of digital conversion of print images into data forms that can be manipulated or that become obsolete exemplify the enduring ephemerality of digital memory, the tension at the core of digital media haunted by processes of obsolescence and regeneration. Defining the digital as the enduring ephemeral, Chun problematizes the conflation of digital memory with long-term storage, drawing attention instead to digital content as "constantly disseminated and regenerated" and, like embodied performance, depending on circulation and transfer for its durability.

Expressions such as "viral spread" and "hashtag exhaustion" foreground the temporal dimension of hashtags as enduring ephemerals that connect rapid-fire social media intensity with the processes of memory and re-emergence that pulsating performance constellations make visible and exploit. Placed as modifiers in social media posts, hashtags allow movements to capitalize on emergence (viral spread) and on processes of ephemerality (hashtag exhaustion) and regeneration. When activists resurface or reactivate declining or exhausted hashtags to address new developments in connection with issues that had lost momentum, they initiate a new beat in an unfolding constellation. Working with the passing (changing, unstable, vanishing) and the repetitive dynamics that characterize digital memory as enduring impermanence, contemporary activists transform images into events (as in the case of the *Time* magazine cover) and charged reactions into the developing processes of affective intensity that feed social mobilization (as in #SavingMexico-#SlayingMexico). This is what makes contemporary social movements pulsating performance constellations supported by the enduring ephemerality of hashtags.

FROM #YAMECANSE (IAMTIRED) TO #USTIRED2: MOBILIZING EXHAUSTION

The hashtag #YaMeCanse (#IAmTired, #IveHadEnough), created in response to a statement made by Mexico's attorney general, Jesús Murillo Karam, at a press conference set to provide news about the search for the Ayotzinapa students, illustrates the process through which activists negotiate the waves of intensity (as well as the emerging forms of control) that accumulate around hashtags on a temporal line. #YaMeCanse illustrates how a viral event responding to a local conflict may become a sustained gesture, transforming censorship into an opportunity to connect sites affected by systemic, institutional violence.

As mentioned earlier, in the weeks that followed the Ayotzinapa students' kidnapping in Iguala, investigators discovered mass graves daily. For example, on October 4, eight days after the Iguala incidents, authorities found twenty-eight bodies in four mass graves, while the Mexican people still waited for President Peña Nieto, who was in China negotiating trade deals, to address the students' disappearance. On October 11, authorities communicated their relief, declaring that the remains found in the mass graves did not belong to the Ayotzinapa students. However, understandably, this escalated rather than placated the Ayotzinapa crisis as the remains from unidentified victims of violence reenergized a public recognition of the severity of the country's narco violence crisis. Or, rather, this incident broke the previous state of acceptance of dead bodies as "collateral damage" of the War on Drugs initiated by President Felipe Calderón in 2006.

Building on popular indignation over these discoveries of mass graves, #Ayotzinapa as an evolving event reached a new tipping point when on November 7, 2014, Attorney General Murillo Karam announced that he believed the students had been found, although their remains were unidentifiable because the students' bodies had been burned and thrown into a river. At the end of a long press conference, believing that his mic was off, Murillo Karam stated, "Ya me cansé" (I've had enough). This phrase, intended to end the dialogue with the press, was resignified on Twitter by activists who turned the hashtag #YaMeCanse into Mexico's trending topic and labored to sustain it as part of a potentially catalyzing moment. In response to the dismissive statement used by the attorney general to shut down the public questioning, activists launched #YaMeCanse to put an end to the state's inaction and its complacency with organized crime.

Accruing four million mentions, #YaMeCanse was featured as Mexico's trending topic over the course of twenty-six days. The hashtag became a collective cry by which the Mexican people expressed their rejection of the official discourse concerning the Ayotzinapa case. Moreover, #YaMeCanse conveyed people's determination to put a stop to the recurrence of death and terror dominating the country's public sphere and their potent will to catalyze a deep transformation of Mexican democracy.

As the #YaMeCanse hashtag gained momentum accumulating dissent, its sudden vanishing from the trending topics list led activists to suspect that the government had transferred the disappearance strategy online.[34] Speculating that a spam bot attack had "drowned" the hashtag to placate

Figure 9: #IAmTired meme, circulated in response to the discovery of mass graves in multiple sites in late 2014.

social mobilization and censor the movement, social media activists quickly responded.[35] They added the number 2 (and then 3 and so on until reaching number 18) to #YaMeCanse to sidestep the networked repression and continue gathering support for the movement.[36]

Following the confrontation that took #YaMeCanse as a site of struggle, activists reconverted #YaMeCanse2 into #USTired2. With this hashtag, Latino/a activists and sympathizers embarked on the task of engaging the US public on- and offline in marches and rallies. Framed by this hashtag and motto, protests for Ayotzinapa were carried out in more than forty cities in the United States. #USTired2 was employed as a transborder tool to spread news about the Ayotzinapa kidnappings alongside critical awareness of the role of the United States in financing the failed war on drugs in Mexico. As Octavio Guerra states, the US-launched Mérida Initiative has funded an expansion of the Mexican state that works to safeguard foreign investment and extraction through military and paramilitary interventions.[37]

Moreover, #USTired2 became a truly transnational signifier when it was inserted into tweets engaging the December 14, 2014, march in New York City after a grand jury declined to indict the NYPD officer who choked Staten Island resident Eric Garner to death.[38] In this context, #USTired2 enabled activists in the United States to express transnational solidarity with the families of the disappeared students, to denounce the US accountability in narco violence in Mexico, and to link the Ayotzinapa campaign to activism against systemic racism and police violence.

At the end of 2014, Mexican and Latina/o activists also employed the hashtag #Fergusinapa and similar protest tactics to reach US and international audiences with news about the forced disappearance of the forty-three students. In the wake of the acquittal of the police officer who murdered Mike Brown in Ferguson, Missouri, #Fergusinapa was not merely an opportunistic gesture deployed by activists in order to insert an international issue in the local news agenda.[39] Rather, #Fergusinapa was an example of hemispheric resistance that highlights the continuity of forms and ideologies of colonial power in present day neoliberal political economies that deem marginalized and resistant bodies as disposable.[40] Through the use of hashtags as statements of alliance and solidarity, activists wove together on- and offline acts of resistance, bringing attention to shared histories of oppression in the Americas.

#INTHEEVENTOFPERFORMANCE

As these examples show, hashtags galvanize responses to evolving events, transforming them into trending topics and anchors of hemispheric memory and resistance. As both ephemeral and persistent mechanisms, hashtags play a critical role in social movements' struggles against symbolic and material erasure. As enduring ephemerals, hashtags materialize a notion of the event of performance as disruption and becoming, enabling instances of real-time reaction, resurgence, and recurrence that help sustain movements across time and space. Through the iteration of hashtag use and their indexical, aggregative, affective features, the short-lived intensity of hashtags (particularly as they escalate to the trending topic category) is repurposed in order to connect various moments within a campaign and to give texture to social mobilizations by linking them transnationally.

In the Mexican context discussed here, hyperlinked hashtags enabled social media users to transcend the short-span choreography of "trending" and to map out multiplicity in extended time-space. Besides featuring tactics of intensity and accumulation, hashtags in the Ayotzinapa campaign configured pulsating performance constellations that mobilized tactics of persistence and political reinvention. Activists productively built on the degeneration and regeneration processes at play within digital culture, composing recursive appearances that extended agonistic, counterhegemonic performances beyond ephemeral virality.

As Van Dijck explains, Twitter's trending topics category epitomizes the platform's valorization of intensity over quality. "Trending" signals both "streams of heavily circulated messages" (measured in tweets per second) and "content-messages" that seek to make a message viral and thus "jump the fence" beyond specific platforms and publics. As I explained earlier, influencers are better positioned to create a trend by prompting virality. That is why, by rewarding intensity over quality, and by scripting the terms in which a tweet bears more weight than others through algorithmic choreographies, Twitter favors a hierarchical user base rather than the presumed, evenly distributed, democratic social media sphere praised by social media advocates.[41]

Even as these findings complicate notions of agency and impact in digitally mediated activism, revealing how Twitter "masks a cacophony of push and pulls forces," as argued by Van Dijck, these facts support my argument that what turns rapid-fire, algorithmically propelled platforms such as Twitter into tools for sustaining mobilization is the symbolic labor of activists who weave ephemeral networked activity into longer dramaturgies of pulsating collective action. Here we can redefine activist performance or structured, iterated, mobilizing behavior as a sort of algorithm in itself, a mode of vanishing that bears the capacity to return.

In this contemporary moment, when hegemonic powers base their legitimacy on their control of media monopolies, as exemplified by the Mexican case and others that readers might resonate with, hashtags are text-based performances that "do things" both as gut-fired reactions to breaking news and as sustained, recurrent interventions that aim to bring forth spaces of resistance and subjective transformation.

As networked iterative or citational practices with worldmaking effects, hashtags are performative. Hashtags epitomize the culture of networked, coordinated effort that we studied in previous chapters, bringing together tactics of synchronic convergence, global and local resonance, and asynchronous cooperation. They are vital examples of distributed democracies that foster processes of counterpower in a moment in which transnational governance and corporate lobbying weakens democratic life.[42]

Even though hashtags are part of corporate infrastructures and subject to new forms of state censorship and control as well as appropriation and reversal by reactionary movements, the importance of hashtags in contemporary progressive social movements cannot be underestimated. They offer a fruitful site for the investigation of networked processes of civic engagement and insurgent mobilization in response to deadly regimes of power. Integrally related to the task of galvanizing moments into persistent movements, hashtags contribute their flickering and insistent performance to a pulsating constellation of forms of activism that seek to contest social erasure and cultivate seeds of social change.[43]

Conclusion

Together We Are Infinite:
Projecting Performance Constellations

When news broke out in August 2016 about the release of "Belén,"[1] the twenty-seven-year-old woman who was imprisoned on allegations of having an abortion, Argentinian journalist Marta Dillon tweeted: "Juntas somos infinitas" (Together we are infinite). With this phrase, Dillon, a member of the feminist collective Ni Una Menos, celebrated the successful culmination of a campaign that had brought together human rights activists, feminists, and social justice militants. Belén's two-year imprisonment in the northwestern province of Tucumán, Argentina, began when she was taken from the hospital where she had sought medical attention for a hemorrhage to jail in the early hours of the morning on March 21, 2014. Just a few days before a new anniversary of the March 26, 1976, coup Belén's arrest at the hospital evoked the abductions carried out by paramilitary forces during the last dictatorship, prompting associations between past and present forms of state-sponsored violence.

Highly circulated phrases such as #LiberenABelen and "A Belén la sacamos entre todas" (#FreeBelen and Together we will free Belén) kept social mobilization going for months. Multiple efforts steered by the consortium Mesa para la Libertad de Belén energized the #FreeBelen campaign.[2] Activists coordinated marches, Twitter storms, and events in collaboration with the well-established Campaña Nacional por el Derecho al Aborto Legal, Seguro y Gratuito (National Campaign for the Right to Legal, Safe and Free Abortion), a feminist initiative launched in 2005.[3] The #Free-Belen activist constellation also included organizations fighting for the continuity of the program for Educación Sexual Integral (Integrative Sexual Education) amid the region's neoconservative turn and the massive budget cuts implemented by the then recently elected president, Mauricio Macri.[4]

Clearly, neither a hashtag nor a tweet freed Belén. But those lines of convergence and dissemination, intersection and flight that configure the # sign have a lot to do, symbolically and materially, with Dillon's assertion that "together we are infinite." The hashtag sign allegorizes the contemporary paradigm of social media-propelled political activation; it is the most visible expression and mechanism of coalition-building processes that are reinvigorated by distributed forms of activism. Besides emphasizing the power of collectivity—like its famous predecessor, "The people united will never be defeated"—"Together we are infinite" celebrates and affirms that the power of collectivity cannot be measured nor exhausted; it is limitless, unbounded, incommensurable. "Together we are infinite" replaces the monolithic, bounded notion of "the people" with a diversified and contingent whole—a unity that is always in the throes of dialectical processes, regroupings, expanding inclusion, and change.[5]

Digital networks and performance as platforms of expressive, embodied, and symbolic behavior are core tools in this dialectical process between convergence and dissemination, leader-based organizing and decentered activation, that I have been calling performance constellations. As figures of relation that articulate dispersed, multisited, and asynchronous forms of collective action, performance constellations are the expression and motor of "infinite togetherness."

Fast forward to 2018: two years after Belén's case galvanized public opinion, the motto of the National Campaign for the Right to Legal, Safe, and Free Abortion (La Campaña), "Sex education to decide, contraceptives to not abort, legal abortion to not die," invades Buenos Aires and other Argentine cities. The proabortion rights' symbol, the green scarf modeled on the iconic white headscarf used by the Mothers of Plaza de Mayo since 1977,[6] has become part of everyday life, worn by longtime and newly arrived activists on their wrists, necks, and particularly on their backpacks. Green-adorned backpacks signal, unequivocally, the massification of the prochoice campaign, particularly after teenagers, one of the groups most affected by laws that hinder reproductive health rights, took on the fight and organized in schools and other social venues.

Just as hashtags such as #NiUnaMenos and #VivasNosQueremos, La Campaña's green scarf is a material artifact that represents and facilitates the experiences of mediated togetherness propelling contemporary social movements. Whereas in the late seventies the Mothers of Plaza de Mayo wore white scarves on their heads to symbolize their missing children's diapers during their rounds across from the government palace under military surveillance, in 2018 reproductive rights demonstrators *unfold* their green scarves and place them in contiguity to each other during protest

Figure 10: Protesters spread their green scarves representing reproductive rights during the Ni Una Menos annual demonstration in Buenos Aires on June 4, 2018. Photo courtesy of Sol Vazquez.

events.[7] Known as *pañuelazos* (or *scarfazos* in English-speaking contexts) this "greening" of public spaces creates a uniform presence out of little fragments, leaving the loose end of a green scarf as an open invitation (a node that opens a new vector) and thus materializing the infinite unfolding of alliance and solidarity.

Captured in full effect thanks to drone technologies of visualization, scarfazos are disseminated via the internet and mainstream media to provide evidence of massive popular support in the demand to legalize abortion and put pressure on decision-makers as the law Voluntary Interruption of Pregnancy is debated in the legislature. The images of massive vigils in cities such as Buenos Aires and Córdoba are complemented by *scarfazos* tactically staged to intensify the presence of smaller crowds or to literally bridge distant locations in provinces with less popular support or more control by the church and the ruling elites.

Scarfazos were also carried out in New York and other cities of the United States and Europe to show international solidarity. Latin American countries such as Bolivia, Peru, and Costa Rica also performed protests in alliance, adopting the green scarf to propel reproductive rights laws in their own localities.[8] The sustained presence of abortion rights' supporters in the streets was repeatedly cited as part of prochoice arguments favoring the law as it was debated in the house of representatives on June 13, and later in the senate on August 8.[9]

Figure 11: This green tide meme was heavily circulated on social media in mid-June 2018 during the abortion rights' debate in Congress.

Pañuelazos were of course complemented by social media activity where featured hashtags such as #QueSeaLey (#LetItBeLegal) as a demand to state representatives turned into #SeraLey (#ItWillBeLegal) as a hopeful projection *and* a performative doing of collective self-determination. Through #SeraLey, and with an understanding of the affective force of coalitional, multiplatform efforts, activists manifested their awareness of the revolutionary role they played in the process of broadening rights for women and *personas gestantes*.[10] Mirroring the way in which Twitter algorithms turn rapid-fire hashtag use into trending topics,[11] #SeraLey communicated a belief in popular sovereignty, and in social change as the effect of sustained popular mobilization. This empowered self-perception of the developing feminist movement in Argentina was depicted in memes that featured a green ocean wave about to engulf the dome of the Congress Palace. Memetic, viral representations of the sovereign green wave made vivid what #SeraLey communicated textually.

Although the proposed legalization of abortion failed in 2018, the mobilization continues. In a country like Argentina, with a strong tradition of popular mobilization and human rights activism, the so-called green tide is not merely a trend or a moment but part of a sustained and *sustaining* history of citizen activism.[12] *La revolución de las pibas* (the girls' revolution)—or *la revolución de las hijas de Ni Una Menos* (the revolution of the daughters of Ni Una Menos), as feminist journalists called the expanded 2018 campaign for reproductive rights—marks how past, present, and future accumulate to effect social justice. The Mothers of Plaza de Mayo, the women who became crucial actors in the Movement of Unemployed Workers and neighborhood assemblies in post-2001 Argentina, the leaders of La Campaña who framed abortion as a health policy issue, the National Women's Meetings where La Campaña emerged, LGBTQ activists, or the "normative gender-sex diaspora," as feminist scholar Dora Barrancos calls them, and, of course, the activists of the Ni Una Menos collective, all form the foundation and motor of this movement. This is a feminist performance constellation that has accumulated over four decades *and* spanned great distances as it articulates local, national, and international forms of togetherness in the streets, political and educational institutions, and the Net.

"Together we are infinite," "the green tide," *scarfazos*, and other discursive and bodily performances of collectivity exemplify a feminist understanding of body politics beyond individual, clearly demarcated bodies, such as those fostered by the neoliberal rhetoric of self-improvement, individual effort, and meritocracy. These are forms of furthering and manifesting a "becoming collective," that is, constellative dramaturgies in which particular circumstances and needs are not approached as the symptom of personal shortcomings or "mistakes" but of systemic oppression and exploitation. These figures of relation, that is, these differently shaped and expressed performance constellations, weave what political philosopher Jodi Dean calls "disintegrated spectacles" to constitute tides, earth-shaking collective screams, and potentially infinite, incommensurable formations.[13]

Each of the constellations that we followed in this book demonstrates that performance and digital networking are crucial resources in present-day struggles for social transformation. They are critical components in the task of organizing the expression of a movement as well as in making its organization *expressive*. As visual artist and theorist Hito Steyerl contends, the symbolic level of demonstrations, their expressive language (images, dogmas, passions), shapes the structural organization and the political force of movements. For Steyerl, the political significance of movements, campaigns, and protests is derived from their form of articulation, from the way in which they link demands, self-obligations, and priorities together with concatenations of different coalitions.[14] That is, activist performances, on- and offline, are not just spectacular but performative; they enact and create transformative conditions.

However, as daily examples demonstrate, neither performance nor digital networking guarantees progressive politics or effects. Writing in 2009 before the intensification of networked communication through social media culture, Dean claims that digital communication media breeds what she calls "communicative capitalism," that is, "a plethora of contestations [that] hinder the formation of a strong counterhegemonic form."[15] Resonating with the debates that took place in the late nineties within the alterglobalization movement, Dean is part of the dystopian intellectual camp that questions the real effects of both street and networked acts of dissent, particularly in the United States, where "criticism does not stick as criticism" but rather as content circulation without consequence.[16]

The examples this book has engaged with show ample proof to the contrary; they demonstrate that multilayered, sustained, local, and transnational protests and activisms do mobilize counterhegemonic, grassroots forms of power building. As articulations of demands, claims, and means, the activist constellations I analyzed in this book are enactments of the political—which Dean defines as "the terrain upon which claims to universality are raised and defended"—as claims that extend beyond oneself to consider structural conditions and possibilities for transformation.[17]

In this sense, as I have shown, activist performance constellations disrupt neoliberal consensus and legitimation, articulating demands that concern the common good. Although they do not guarantee progressive politics in themselves, in the contexts we have explored in this book, performance constellations have been instrumental to those affected by the exploitative, individualizing, and mutating forces of neoliberalism. Through them, protesters have challenged neoliberal forms of governance that, as Judith Butler claims, demand self-sufficiency while making it impossible to attain.[18]

The tactics of online convergence, local-global articulation, movement expansion, and persistence facilitated by performance constellations contributed to the Zapatistas' survival at the height of the Mexican government's military repression of their insurgence, solidified the alterglobalization movement driven by compelling practices of grassroots democracy, and disrupted citizens' complacency with indebtedness and state violence in parasitic and extractive transnational political economies. Performance constellations provide emerging modalities of "being against" and "being together" that reinvigorate severely compromised democracies through practices of agonism that challenge neoliberal consensus.

To be sure, because the performance constellations I mapped here are geographically and historically specific, the question becomes: are these tactics of collective mobilization and political engagement transferrable? Are they not dependent on particular legacies and contemporary cultures of popular mobilization and collaboration? On the contrary, however, as I showed, examples of actions that take place within performance constellations employ shared knowledge and expressive tropes in well-rooted yet remarkably flexible ways, demonstrating the adaptability and historicity of an emergent transnational culture. Examples such as EDT's virtual sit-ins, the Chilean students' use of the flash mob classic *Thriller*, and the circulation of pots-and-pans protests illustrate the modalities of crosspollination, citationality, and contextual adaptation that create performance constellations as acts of memory transfer that keep on changing.[19] As Steyerl claims, the articulation of protests through their expressive form is necessary for their globalization. And this articulation, I would add, recreates the function of local protest performances as ways of decoding, revealing, and intervening in transnational systems of governance.

Perhaps the biggest lesson offered by *Performance Constellations* is that, drawing from both performance and digital media's "never for the first time" ontologies,[20] contemporary activisms in Latin America break from hegemonic orders that aim to legitimize violence and oppression, and they also enact popular sovereignty and/as the foundation for social justice. As I have argued here, what performance constellations as multilayered forms of activism and protest do best is to enable collective acts that seek to challenge the power that sustains hegemonic orders. As embodied, networked modes of political appearance, performance constellations put bodies center stage to reclaim the value of life and denounce socioeconomic inequality as the calculated outcome of death-creating systems of exploitation.

I do not mean to imply that the streets and digital networks are guaranteed means of resistance, or that they will always be at our disposal as activist platforms. We know that repressive administrations can easily shut down street protests as well as social media; we know as well that many, including trans folks, women of color, and undocumented people, cannot risk detention, while others remain without access to technology. That is why I hope the analytic deconstruction of performance tactics that I deployed here inspires readers to assess situated conditions and tools and take the course of action that best suits their circumstances. As tactical media activists claimed, we need to be "always on the move." By reconstructing how activists in Chile, Mexico, and Argentina articulated tactics of dissent even in extremely challenging and chaotic contexts, I hope this book energizes activists, artists, and scholars, to extrapolate what they have learned in these pages and apply it to their own critical contexts, understanding that, as I have argued, the performance constellations we followed focus on both macro and micro disruptions, on collective mobilization and individual desubjectivation, and on political, social, and cultural change.

Our current state of capitalist acceleration that has led to the displacement and extreme vulnerability of migrants, refugees, and the disenfranchised, and that has weakened democracies while empowering elites, extreme right-wing organizations, and criminal networks, suggests an uncertain future. Social media are indeed one of the environments where toxic networks breed, disagreement is met with harassment, and civic dialogue is circumscribed to an echo chamber of "friending" and "unfriending."[21] In fact, sadly, in the late 2010s it is right-wing and fundamentalist groups who are dispelling all doubts about digital networks as radical social mobilization platforms.

Further, recent revelations about Russian trolls posing as Black Lives Matter activists or disgruntled Democrat supporters fleeing the party, seem to give a clear indication that social media activism is not categorically trustworthy.[22] The famous statement by a four-legged creature in Peter Stein's 1993 *New Yorker* cartoon that "on the Internet, nobody knows you are a dog" is eerily updated twenty-five years later, at a moment in which it is unclear who (or what) influences election results.

While there are serious counterforces at work against the movements and the tactics I describe and advocate for in this book (disinformation campaigns, data mining, spam attacks, and troll squads' mimicry, for example), performance constellations demonstrate how activists and artists develop counterpower protocols to navigate the challenges brought about by technologies of pervasive surveillance, control, and manipulation. The emergent threats brought about by governments' and other agencies' uses of digital networks to demobilize or disorient networked publics make the study of performance as a multiplatform, human and posthuman phenomenon all the more urgent.

Despite these challenges, however, I find it difficult to carry on living without hope. And *hope* is what moved the activists and protesters that we engaged with here. Their hope for better futures and their determination to create them started with an active commitment to end the enforced consensus and normalization of violence that sustain policies detrimental to more and more people each day. As we saw in the example of Mexican protesters when they stated, "They didn't know we were seeds," emancipatory activism breaks conditions of uncontested injustice and puts change in motion. Phrases such as "Together we are infinite" turn "They didn't know we were seeds" into "*We* didn't know we were seeds." "Together we are infinite" is not simply an assertion; it's a realization that becomes possible only after the act. This phrase teaches us that performance constellations do not only represent our strength; they create it, making it tangible and concrete to us and to hegemonic forces.

The performance constellations that breathe here prove that it was once possible to work for change and that these seeds (or stars) can still be reanimated—as long as we have what it takes to bring them back to life. That is the promise of ephemeral performances and assemblies: they end, they start again. Many are emerging right this minute; other, like the Zapatista practices of self-governance, go on steadily, or unfold like border-crossing green scarves. This book and the activists featured in it have given us tools. Now we must look forward with the knowledge and memory of these stories. And get to work.

Notes

INTRODUCTION

1. See Fernando Calderón, coord., "Understanding Social Conflict in Latin America," United Nations Development Programme, Fundación UNIR, Bolivia, 2013; Christina Schatzman, "Political Challenge in Latin America: Rebellion and Collective Protest in an Era of Democratization," *Journal of Peace Research* 42.3 (2005): 291–310; and Sonia Alvarez et al., eds., *Beyond Civil Society: Activism, Participation and Protest in Latin America* (Durham, NC: Duke University Press, 2017).

2. I learned about this when I asked Teresa Sarrail, a professor of drama at Universidad Nacional de las Artes, the history of the building of the National Drama Conservatory during my 2016 visit to Buenos Aires.

3. In Argentina, the theater community has played a crucial role, marking the end of obedience to the dictators and initiating the transition to democracy. For example, as Brenda Werth notes, the two first iterations of the theater festival Teatro Abierto (Open Theater, 1981–1985) functioned as "a collective theatrical act of resistance in defiance of the dictatorship." Because of the festival's bold positioning vis-à-vis censorship and state terror, the Picadero Theater, where Teatro Abierto took place, was consequently bombed in the early morning of August 6, 1981. See Brenda Werth, *Theatre, Performance, and Memory Politics in Argentina* (New York: Palgrave Macmillan, 2010).

4. On protest as radical performance, see Baz Kershaw, *The Radical in Performance: Between Brecht and Baudrillard* (London: Routledge, 1999).

5. Jodi Dean claims that, in a context of media saturation where everyone is a prosumer, that is, both a consumer and a producer of content, "messages get lost," becoming mere occasions for processes of indefinite circulation that create what Dean terms "communicative capitalism." See *Democracy and Other Neoliberal Fantasies: Communicative Capitalism and Left Politics* (Durham, NC: Duke University Press, 2009).

6. In his study of technology in performance, Chris Salter uses the term "entanglement" to define ways in which technology does not complement but transforms artistic practices, challenging the boundaries between human and nonhuman action. See *Entangled: Technology and the Transformation of Performance* (Cambridge, MA: MIT Press, 2010). Whereas Salter's study mainly concerns physically based performance, I use the concept of entanglement to theorize the interaction between on- and offline tactics that generate performance constellations of transnational activism.

7. Readers interested in the concept of "constellation" in cultural studies might want to consult Norm Friesen, "Wandering Star: The Image of the Constellation in Benjamin, Giedion, and McLuhan," July 2013, http://www.academia.edu/4032277/Wandering_Star_The_Image_of_the_Constellation_in_Benjamin_Giedion_and_McLuhan. For a performance-oriented approach, see Lynette Hunter, "Constellation: Engaging with Radical Devised Dance Theatre. Keith Henessy's *Sol Niger*," in *Performance, Politics, and Activism*, edited by John Rouse and Peter Lichtenfels (New York: Palgrave Macmillan, 2013), 132–153.

8. On the notion of affective circulation, see Sara Ahmed, "Affective Economies," *Social Text* 22.2 (2004): 117–139.

9. See Kershaw, *The Radical in Performance*, and Susan Leigh Foster, "Choreographies of Protest," *Theatre Journal* 55.3 (2003): 395–412.

10. Françoise Lionnet and Shu-mei Shih explain that, whereas the global is "a homogenous and dominant set of criteria, the transnational designates spaces and practices acted upon by border-crossing agents, be they dominant or marginal." These theorists situate transnationalism as a consequence of the latest wave of globalization. They state that transnationalism and globalization belong to the phase of advanced capitalism defined by practices of financial investment, flexible accumulation, and post-Fordist labor circuits and that while transnationalism is "part and parcel of globalization . . . it can be less scripted and more scattered." See Françoise Lionnet and Shu-mei Shih, eds., *Minor Transnationalism* (Durham, NC: Duke University Press, 2005), 5.

11. In this sentence, I play with Peggy Phelan's oft-cited definition of performance as an art form that "becomes itself through disappearance," meaning that ephemerality is foundational to the politics of performance as a nonreproductive form. See *Unmarked: The Politics of Performance* (London: Routledge, 1993), 146.

12. Here I engage with the debate between scholars who define performance as an ephemeral act or event that is always new, that is, ontologically nonreproducible (Peggy Phelan) and those who claim that performance is a system of memory, a cultural reservoir (Richard Schechner, Joseph Roach, Diana Taylor). José Esteban Muñoz and Fred Moten claim that the ephemerality of performance is actually a precondition for its reproducibility, and that what we might call performance's flickering status is crucial to minoritarian subjects escaping hypervisibility as a form of social control and dehumanization. See Muñoz, "Ephemera as Evidence: Introductory Notes to Queer Acts," *Women and Performance* 8.2 (1996): 5–17; and Moten, *In the Break: The Aesthetics of the Black Radical Tradition* (Minneapolis: University of Minnesota Press, 2003).

13. Jonathan Matthew Smucker defines prefigurative politics as a philosophy that "seeks to demonstrate the 'better world' it envisions for the future in the actions it takes today" (103). Smucker sets prefigurative politics in contraposition to "power politics" directed to influence long-term change. Conversely, Benjamin Arditi, argues that prefigurative politics, which he defines as "political performatives," is already transformative of the world (and of politics) as we know it. See Smucker, *Hegemony How-To: A Roadmap for Radicals* (Baltimore: AK Press, 2017); and Arditi, "Insurgencies Don't Have a Plan— They *Are* the Plan: Political Performatives and Vanishing Mediators," in *The*

Promise and Perils of Populism: Global Perspectives, edited by Carlos de la Torre (Lexington: University Press of Kentucky, 2014), 113–139.

14. Linda Kauffman argues that the 1970s antinuclear movement is a breaking point in the history of social mobilization in the United States because it created "a new model for large-scale actions" that embodied "a new way of living and acting." Kauffman states that this model became widespread at a moment when change became particularly hard to envision. Thus, Kauffman teaches us that prefigurative politics are always contextual and should be assessed by taking into consideration the conditions, tools, and systems available to activists to envision and work toward social change. See *Direct Action: Protest and the Reinvention of American Radicalism* (London: Verso Books, 2017). For a performance-focused discussion about social change, see Stephani Etheridge Woodson and Tamara Underiner, eds., *Theatre, Performance and Change* (Cham, Switzerland: Palgrave Macmillan, 2018).

15. #YoSoy132 was a social mobilization prompted by a group of 131 students that confronted Mexican president Enrique Peña Nieto during his visit to the Ibero-American University on May 11, 2012. After Peña Nieto accused the protesters of being infiltrators, students created a YouTube video showing their university IDs. Supporters used the hashtag #YoSoy132 to back the students. This initiated a civic movement that denounced mass-media manipulation and corporate influence in electoral politics.

16. See, particularly, Zizi Papacharissi, *Affective Publics: Sentiment, Technology, and Politics* (Oxford: Oxford University Press, 2014); and Lisa Kember and Joanna Zylinska, *Life after New Media: Mediation as a Vital Process* (Cambridge, MA: MIT Press, 2014).

17. Years later, Facebook users would reminisce on this event and state that it would be great to re-perform it, as students had not achieved their goal yet. Replayed through Facebook memories, the flash mob reminded spectators of the 2011 protest cycle and compelled them to return to the fight, using algorithmic performance to highlight unfinished business.

18. Verónica Gago, *Neoliberalism from Below: Popular Pragmatics and Baroque Economies*, translated by Liz Mason-Desee (Durham, NC: Duke University Press, 2017).

19. Paolo Gerbaudo, *Tweets and the Streets: Social Media and Contemporary Activism* (London: Pluto; New York: distributed in the United States by Palgrave Macmillan, 2012).

20. Dance scholar Susan Leigh Foster offers choreography as an analytic to highlight the symbolic and material function of the body as an activist tool. Building on Foster's work, Paolo Gerbaudo coins the term "choreographies of assembly" to characterize how organizers use social media to "set the stage" for crucial face-to-face assemblies. See Foster, "Choreographies of Protest" and Gerbaudo, *Tweets and the Streets*.

21. In fact, Margaret Thatcher's support of Pinochet's policies was crucial to the continuity of neoliberalism in Chile. Thatcher maintained her alliance to the dictator even after his 1998 indictment and arrest in London for human rights violations.

22. David Harvey, *A Brief History of Neoliberalism* (New York: Oxford University Press, 2005), 7.

23. Ibid., 2. On neoliberalism as governmental rationality and generalized logic spanning from states to subjectivity, see Pierre Dardot and Christian Laval, *The New Way of the World: On Neoliberal Society* (London: Verso, 2014).

24. Adam Smith, *The Wealth of Nations: Books I–IV*. Edited by Andrew Skinner (London: Penguin Books, 1999).

25. Lisa Duggan, *The Twilight of Equality? Neoliberalism, Cultural Politics, and the Attack on Democracy* (Boston: Beacon Press, 2003).

26. Ibid., xii.

27. Harvey, *Brief History of Neoliberalism*, 2.

28. Arlene Dávila argues that Latin Americans introduced the topic of neoliberalism in American studies scholarship. Focusing on how neoliberal regimes in Latin America determine the value and function of culture, Dávila cautions against approaching neoliberalism as "a thing" rather than a deeply contextual process. See Arlene Dávila, "Locating Neoliberalism in Time, Space, and 'Culture,'" *American Quarterly* 66.3 (2014): 549–555.

29. For an account of Salvador Allende's cybernetic socialist project, see Eden Medina, *Cybernetic Revolutionaries: Technology and Politics in Allende's Chile* (Cambridge, MA: MIT Press, 2011).

30. See Juan José Carrillo Nieto, "El neoliberalismo en Chile: Entre la legalidad y la legitimidad. Entrevista a Tomás Moulián," *Perfiles Latinoamericanos* 1.35 (January 1, 2010): 145–155; and Naomi Klein, *The Shock Doctrine: The Rise of Disaster Capitalism* (New York: Picador, 2007).

31. Gago, *Neoliberalism from Below*.

32. In actuality, in the 1960s and 1970s, popular and student movements that challenged the single-party rule were persecuted by counterinsurgency programs administered by generals trained in the School of the Americas. During the Mexican "Dirty War" (1968–1982) more than twelve hundred people were disappeared by force.

33. See Chris Gilbreth and Gerardo Otero, "Democratization in Mexico: The Zapatista Uprising and Civil Society," *Latin American Perspectives* 28.4 (July 2001): 7–29.

34. See Marcela A. Fuentes, "#NiUnaMenos (#NotOneWomanLess): Hashtag Performativity, Memory, and Direct Action against Gender Violence in Argentina," in *Women Mobilizing Memory*, edited by Ayse Gul Altinay, Maria José Contreras, Zeynep Gambetti, and Alisa Solomon (New York: Columbia University Press, 2019), 172–191.

35. In both Chile and Argentina in the 1990s, during democratic administrations neoliberalism intensified. In Chile, the relative success of Pinochet's economic program created a climate of political apathy through the idea that political deactivation had paid off. See María José Contreras Lorenzini, "A Woman Artist in the Neoliberal Chilean Jungle," in *Performance, Feminism and Affect in Neoliberal Times*, edited by Elin Diamond, Denise Varney, and Candice Amich (London: Palgrave Macmillan, 2017), 239–251.

36. Hannah Arendt, *The Human Condition* (Chicago: University of Chicago Press, 1958).

37. Duggan, *The Twilight of Equality*, xii.

38. As Judith Butler notes, Arendt's notion of the space of appearance is based on the Greek polis that separates the public and the private and privi-

leges public speaking as political over the body as a site of unfreedom based on needs. Engaging contemporary forms of oppression, Butler underscores embodiment as a political ground. Writing about the performative workings and effects of street assemblies, Butler defines "gathering" as a way of reestablishing the space of appearance for "those associated with bodily existence" (women, children, the exploited, and so on) to make manifest their "differential exposure to death." Judith Butler, *Notes toward a Performative Theory of Assembly* (Cambridge, MA: Harvard University Press, 2015).

39. Ibid.

40. On race and/ as performance, see E. Patrick Johnson, *Appropriating Blackness: Performance and the Politics of Authenticity* (Durham, NC: Duke University Press, 2003).

41. On the avant-garde origins of a Euro- and US-centric history of performance art, see RoseLee Goldberg, *Performance Art: From Futurism to the Present*, rev. ed. (New York: Thames & Hudson, 2001). For a succinct historiography of performance linking the European avant-garde, Gutai, the 1960s social movements, and Reagan, see Peggy Phelan, "Live Culture: Performance and the Contemporary," Tate Museum, March 29, 2003, http://www.tate.org.uk/context-comment/video/live-culture-performance-and-contemporary-part-1

42. Paul Schimmel, "Leap into the Void: Performance and the Object," in *Out of Actions: Between Performance and the Object, 1949–1979* (London: Thames and Hudson, 1998), 17.

43. Ibid.

44. Luis Camnitzer, *Conceptualism in Latin American Art: Didactics of Liberation* (Austin: University of Texas Press, 2007).

45. Artists used words such as "sabotage," "blackout," "denunciation," *clandestinidad*, "protest," etc., to refer to the delivery or format of their pieces. See Ana Longoni and Mariano Mestman, *Del Di Tella a "Tucumán Arde": Vanguardia artística y política en el '68 argentino* (Buenos Aires: Ediciones El Cielo por Asalto, 2000).

46. For critical surveys of performance art in Latin America, see Coco Fusco, ed., *Corpus Delecti: Performance Art of the Americas* (New York: Routledge, 2000); Cecilia Fajardo-Hill and Andrea Giunta, *Radical Women: Latin American Art, 1960–1985* (Los Angeles: Hammer Museum, University of California; New York: Del Monico Books / Prestel, 2017); and Deborah Cullen, ed., *Arte ≠ Vida: Actions by Artists of the Americas, 1960–2000* (New York: El Museo del Barrio, 2008).

47. Hannah Arendt in *The Phenomenology Reader*, edited by Dermot Moran and Timothy Mooney (New York: Routledge, 2002), 371.

48. Martí Peran, "Arquitectura del Acontecimiento," in *En tiempo real: El arte mientras tiene lugar*, edited by Pedro de Llano and Xosé Lois Gutiérrez (A Coruña: Fundación Luis Seoane, 2001), 117–128.

49. Building on the work of Herbert Blau and Roland Barthes, Phelan links performance to the experience of death and frames spectatorship as witnessing dying. This expands the concept of *liveness* from its use to characterize unmediated aesthetic experiences to highlighting human finitude. Phelan, *Unmarked*, 146.

50. This categorization of performance as event and technology as second order documentation also positions performance in the realm of the here and

now, occluding considerations about embodiment and memory, history, and the archive. Contesting the definition of performance as always for the first time, scholars such as Diana Taylor and Rebecca Schneider position performance as an embodied system of memory and preservation. See Taylor, *The Archive and the Repertoire: Performing Cultural Memory in the Americas* (Durham, NC: Duke University Press, 2003); and Schneider, "Performance Remains," *Performing Research* 6.2 (2001): 100–108.

51. See Steve Dixon, *A History of New Media in Theater, Dance, Performance Art, and Installation* (Cambridge, MA: MIT Press, 2007); and Philip Auslander, "Digital Liveness: A Historico-Philosophical Perspective," *PAJ: A Journal of Performance and Art* 34.3 (2012): 3–11. See also, Sarah Bay-Cheng et al. *Mapping Intermediality in Performance* (Amsterdam: Amsterdam University Press, 2010) and Bay-Cheng, "Digital Culture," in *Performance Studies. Key Words, Concepts and Theories*, edited by Bryan Reynolds (London: Palgrave McMillan, 2014), 39–49.

52. danah boyd, "Participating in the Always-On Lifestyle," in *The Social Media Reader*, edited by Michael Mandiberg (New York: NYU Press, 2012), 71-76.

53. For information about Sastre's performance see the Buenos Aires Performance Biennial website at http://bienalbp.org/bp15/en/martin-sastre/.

54. Esther Weltevrede, Anne Helmond, and Carolin Gerlitz, "The Politics of Real-Time: A Device Perspective on Social Media Platforms and Search Engines," *Theory, Culture & Society* 31.6 (2014): 125–150.

55. Taylor, *Archive and Repertoire*.

56. Jon McKenzie and Rebecca Schneider, "Critical Art Ensemble: Tactical Media Practitioners," *TDR: The Drama Review* 44.4 (2000): 143–144.

57. Rita Raley, *Tactical Media* (Minneapolis: University of Minnesota Press, 2009).

58. This net art piece, no longer active online, can be explored by inputting http://buscarjusticia.linefeed.org/ in the Internet Archive Wayback Machine, https://archive.org/web/

59. See Javier Toret et al., "Tecnopolítica: La potencia de las multitudes conectadas. El sistema red 15M, un nuevo paradigma de la política distribuida," working paper, June 18, 2013, http://tecnopolitica.net/sites/default/files/1878-5799-3-PB%20(2).pdf.

60. *Democracia distribuida: Miradas de la Universidad Nómada al 15M*, Universidad Nómada, 2012, http://www.trasversales.net/ddun15m.pdf.

61. Papacharissi, *Affective Publics*.

62. "Contar la historia de lo que resiste también es una forma de pensar la transformación."

CHAPTER ONE

1. Anna Munster, *Materializing New Media: Embodiment in Information Aesthetics* (Hanover, NH: Dartmouth College Press, 2006), 62.

2. The Critical Art Ensemble (CAE) defined tactical media as a movement that employs the media that are most effective to use to intervene in a particular

context. Neither artists nor political activists in a strict sense, tactical media practitioners "initiate social processes that aid people in perceiving a social system and their roles within it in a manner that is different from the normalized perception of these phenomena." See Jon McKenzie and Rebecca Schneider, "Critical Art Ensemble: Tactical Media Practitioners," *TDR: The Drama Review* 44.4 (2000): 136–150.

3. The EDT's founder, Ricardo Dominguez, took the concept of Electronic Civil Disobedience from the Critical Art Ensemble (CAE), a group he participated in before creating EDT. Drawing from Paul Virilio's theory that capitalist power systems value speed over attachment to physical spaces, CAE argued that traditional forms of civil disobedience had lost their relevance, and that hence activists needed to carry out civil disobedience online. See Critical Art Ensemble, *Electronic Civil Disobedience and Other Unpopular Ideas* (New York: Autonomedia, 1996).

4. Munster, *Materializing New Media*, 18.

5. See Philip Auslander, "Digital Liveness: A Historico-Philosophical Perspective," *PAJ: A Journal of Performance and Art* 34.3 (2012): 3–11; and Munster, *Materializing New Media*, 4.

6. N. Katherine Hayles, *How We Became Posthuman: Virtual Bodies in Cybernetics, Literature, and Informatics* (Chicago: University of Chicago Press, 1999), 4.

7. Ricardo Dominguez in Coco Fusco, "On-Line Simulations/Real-Life Politics: A Discussion with Ricardo Domínguez on Staging Virtual Theatre," *TDR: The Drama Review* 47.2 (2003): 154.

8. See Gabriella Coleman, "The Ethics of Digital Direct Action," *Aljazeera*, September 2011, http://www.aljazeera.com/indepth/opinion/2011/08/20118308455825769.html. See also Coleman, *Hacker, Hoaxer, Whistleblower, Spy: The Many Faces of Anonymous* (Brooklyn, NY: Verso, 2014).

9. Dominguez quoted in Jill Lane, "Digital Zapatistas," *TDR: The Drama Review* 47.2 (2003): 138.

10. Chantal Mouffe differentiates agonism from antagonism, stating that while antagonism is an essential part of pluralist democracies defined by disagreement rather than by consensus, antagonism requires agonism to mobilize the necessary work of challenging hegemony. In Mouffe's view, agonism sets off counterhegemonic politics. She places art practices as vital tools to mobilize agonistic political tasks. See Mouffe, "Artistic Activism and Agonistic Spaces," *Art & Research* 1.2 (Summer 2007): 1–5; and Paulina Tambakaki, "The Tasks of Agonism and Agonism to the Task: Introducing 'Chantal Mouffe: Agonism and the Politics of Passion,'" *parallax* 20.2 (2014): 1–13.

11. Lane, "Digital Zapatistas."

12. Ana Carrigan, "Chiapas: The First Post-modern Revolution?" *Fletcher Forum* 19.1 (Winter–Spring 1995): 71–98.

13. Laura Carlsen, "Armoring NAFTA: The Battleground for Mexico's Future," *NACLA Report on the Americas* 41.5 (2008): 2.

14. See Chris Gilbreth and Gerardo Otero, "Democratization in Mexico: The Zapatista Uprising and Civil Society," *Latin American Perspectives* 28.4 (July 2001): 7–29.

15. The Zapatistas take their name from Emiliano Zapata, a leader of the Mexican revolution at the turn of the twentieth century who fought against the dictatorship of Porfirio Díaz.

16. See Tom Hayden, ed., *The Zapatista Reader* (New York: Thunder's Mouth Press / Nation Books, 2002), 220.

17. The inclusion of a specific indigenous agenda was a matter that appeared in later declarations. The first declaration makes use of a collective "we" that is not tied to a specific group.

18. Diana Taylor, "Dancing with the Zapatistas," in *Dancing with the Zapatistas: Twenty Years Later*, edited by Diana Taylor and Lorie Novak (Durham, NC: Duke University Press; New York: HemiPress, 2015). http://scalar.usc.edu/anvc/dancing-with-the-zapatistas/zapatistas

19. Ibid. On the politics of vulnerability, see also Judith Butler, Zeynep Gambetti, and Leticia Sabsay, eds., *Vulnerability in Resistance* (Durham, NC: Duke University Press, 2016).

20. Disguised as a masked hero to save Mexicans from political and economic crises, Superbarrio Gómez rose to public notoriety from the Mexico City's Neighborhood Assembly (Asamblea de Barrios) organized after the 1985 earthquake. Dressed in his classic wrestling attire, Superbarrio announced his candidacy for the US presidency in 1996, arguing that US politics are so influential on global geopolitics that candidates and voters should not be confined to those born on US territory.

21. Cited in Lane, "Digital Zapatistas," 136.

22. Drawing on 1970s resource mobilization theory, Jonathan Matthew Smucker, Joshua Kahn Russell, and Zack Malitz differentiate between expressive and instrumental action, stating that the former aims to communicate identity while the latter is used as a means to achieve concrete goals. These authors state that, even though the distinction between expressive and instrumental action is important, they are both valuable tactical approaches and should be combined. See "Expressive and Instrumental Actions," in *Beautiful Trouble: A Toolbox for Revolution*, edited by Andrew Boyd and Dave Oswald Mitchell (New York: OR Books, 2012), 232–233.

23. This phrase belongs to the "Fourth Declaration of the Lacandón Jungle," released two years after the Zapatista insurgency when the EZLN called for a national liberation movement: "The flower of the word will not die. The masked face which today has a name may die, but the word which came from the depth of history and the earth can no longer be cut by the arrogance of the powerful." In Hayden, *The Zapatista Reader*, 239.

24. Jacques Rancière, *The Politics of Aesthetics: The Distribution of the Sensible*, translated by Gabriel Rockhill (London: Continuum, 2006).

25. In an article originally published in *The Guardian* in 2001, writer and activist Naomi Klein identified forty-five thousand Zapatista-related websites based in twenty-six countries. Naomi Klein, "The Unknown Icon," in Hayden, *The Zapatista Reader*, 114.

26. Quoted in Roger Burbach, *Globalization and Postmodern Politics: From Zapatistas to High-Tech Robber Barons* (London: Pluto Press, 2001), 143.

27. At the time, the EDT's members were Dominguez, net artist Brett Stalbaum, computer scientist Carmin Karasic, and media scholar Stefan Wray.

28. See "Cyberpower for Piece in Chiapas: Action Alert," https://www.thing.net/~rdom/ecd/anondigcoal.html.

29. This tactic is an extension of the phone jams that Dominguez used to conduct when he collaborated with ACT UP. Phone jams are another critical mass tactic in which protesters call representatives or organizations identified as responsible parties in a given conflict. By keeping the line busy and also "hijacking" employees who had to answer the phone, these calls sought to disrupt business operations.

30. Dominguez in Jill Lane, "Interview with Ricardo Dominguez," video, Hemispheric Institute of Performance and Politics, Encuentro, Monterrey, Mexico, 2001.

31. Coleman, *Hacker, Hoaxer, Whistleblower, Spy*.

32. As Jonathan Smucker cautions, in order to reach the goal of social justice, we need to focus on tactics as a path to power building and not as an aim in itself. Taking a critical stance toward movements such as Occupy Wall Street, Smucker argues that they fell prey to an in-group fascination with their tactics. However, movements such as the Zapatistas are highly critical of political institutions, and what we perceive as prefigurative politics are actually worldmaking tactics that reinvent politics rather than reinvigorate politics-as-is. See *Hegemony How-To*, chapter 4.

33. Lane bases her analysis on Edward Soja's theorization of spatiality as both the "'embodiment' and medium of social life itself" and on Anne Balsamo's take on virtual embodiment as the effect of a particular "staging" that foregrounds the body as part of a process rather than a fixed entity. See "Digital Zapatistas": 131.

34. Roach uses "kinesthetic imagination" as part of his theorization of performance in embodied processes of memory transmission. He focuses on performance as an ephemeral cultural phenomenon that remains across time and space, particularly in the transnational processes that were part of the slave trade. See *Cities of the Dead: Circum-Atlantic Performance* (New York: Columbia University Press, 1996), 26–27.

35. The body is an important locus of analysis in performance studies. This is due to the body's centrality in performance art and more specifically body art, and to performance studies' focus on culture and social orders as based on symbolic, repeated behavior. Anthropologist Thomas Csordas proposes to broaden our understanding of the body by framing it as "the central ground of culture." This is how Csordas shifts from "body" to "embodiment." This shift entails a move from the body as object of analysis to embodiment as a methodological approach to socially constructed notions such as culture and the self. See Csordas, "Embodiment as a Paradigm for Anthropology," *Ethos* 18.1 (1990): 5–47.

36. See Hayles, *How We Became Posthuman*.

37. Mark B. N. Hansen, *Bodies in Code: Interfaces with New Media* (London: Routledge, 2006).

38. As part of the debate about informational spaces such as the internet as "disembodied," Tara McPherson highlights the feedback loop between analog and digital embodiment. She states that "while the privileged among us might feel closely connected to our digital devices . . . the sensations we feel as we

touch our keyboards and screens are analog feelings, rich in continuous input and gradations of the sensory." See McPherson, "Digital," in *Keywords for American Cultural Studies*, edited by Bruce Burgett and Glenn Hendler, 2nd ed. (New York: New York University Press, 2014), 79–81.

39. Digital activists call this process "swarming."

40. See Manuel Castells's introduction to *The Network Society: A Cross-Cultural Perspective*, edited by Castells (Northampton, MA: Edward Elgar Publishing, 2005).

41. Ibid., 5.

42. Alexander R. Galloway and Eugene Thacker, *The Exploit: A Theory of Networks* (Minneapolis: University of Minnesota Press, 2007), 4.

43. Ibid., 28.

44. Ibid., 29.

45. Ibid., 34.

46. See Anna Munster, *An Aesthesia of Networks: Conjunctive Experience in Art and Technology* (Cambridge, MA: MIT Press, 2013).

47. Capturing the dynamism and flexibility of informational networks, Castells theorizes the internet as the "space of flows" and differentiates it from physical or local space, which he terms the "space of place." The space of flows materializes the possibility of practicing simultaneity without contiguity (as it happens in virtual sit-ins with participants "gathering" on the targeted website despite being in disparate locations). Contrastingly, the space of places is based on practice, experience, and locality, very much in tandem with the canonical definition of theatrical performance as copresence. Although both spaces of flows and spaces of places are defined by social practices, the most crucial operations in our informational society take place in spaces of flows, which are vital environments for financial markets, transnational labor relations, media communication, global governance, and social movements. Castells, *The Network Society*, 36.

48. McKenzie elaborates on Gilles Deleuze and Félix Guattari's notion of the machinic, a term used to explain that machines do not extend or substitute humans but rather conjoin with humans, who are a component of hybrid relations. See Jon McKenzie, "Hacktivism and Machinic Performance," *Performance Paradigm* 1 (March 2005): 22–30. For an elaboration of Deleuze and Guattari's concept of machinic capitalism, see Maurizio Lazzarato, "The Machine," translated by Mary O'Neill, European Institute for Progressive Cultural Politics, http://eipcp.net/transversal/1106/lazzarato/en.

49. HTML stands for "HyperText Markup Language," the computer language used to create web pages. Using the term "conceptualism," the EDT links its digital performance to an artistic period that originated in the 1950s, characterized by works of art in which ideas were more important than aesthetic, sensible dimensions.

50. In "An Inventory of Shimmers," their introduction to *The Affect Theory Reader*, Gregory J. Seigworth and Melissa Greg take on the difficult mission of defining affect. They state that "affect arises in the midst of in-between-ness: in the capacities to act and be acted upon" (1). With this definition, these theorists show how the notion of affect invites us to attend to the force fields that

move us or that suspend us in inaction. See Melissa Greg and Gregory J. Sei-gworth, eds., *The Affect Theory Reader* (Durham, NC: Duke University Press, 2010). See also Brian Massumi, *Parables for the Virtual: Movement, Affect, Sensation* (Durham, NC: Duke University Press, 2002); and Tambakaki, "Tasks of Agonism."

51. Michel de Certeau, *The Practice of Everyday Life*, translated by Stephen F. Rendall (Berkeley: University of California Press, 1984): 37–38.

52. Tactical media's reliance on the logic of intervening in the space of the other or in the law of foreign power without necessarily aiming to overturn hegemonic systems has led scholars to theorize this set of practices as "parasitic" and "incident-based." In that sense, tactics epitomize a "micropolitics of disruption" that favors openness to the unexpected over politically straightforward instrumentalization. See Rita Raley, *Tactical Media* (Minneapolis: University of Minnesota Press, 2009), 9; and Eric Kluitenberg, *Legacies of Tactical Media: The Tactics of Occupation. From Tompkins Square to Tahrir* (Amsterdam: Institute of Network Cultures, 2011), 22.

53. See Kluitenberg, *Legacies of Tactical Media*, 16.

54. Elin Diamond, "Introduction," in *Performance and Cultural Politics*, ed. Diamond (London: Routledge, 1996), 1–12.

55. Joshua Takano Chambers-Letson, *A Race So Different: Performance and Law in Asian America* (New York: New York University Press, 2013), 23.

56. Dominguez in Fusco, "On-Line Simulations," 156. Emphasis mine.

57. Ricardo Dominguez, email communication with the author, December 3, 2006.

58. Walter Benjamin, "What Is Epic Theatre?," in *Illuminations: Essays and Reflections*, edited by Hannah Arendt, translated by Harry Zohn (New York: Schocken Books, 1969).

59. D. Soyini Madison, *Acts of Activism: Human Rights as Radical Performance* (Cambridge: Cambridge University Press, 2010), 220.

60. Augusto Boal, *Theater of the Oppressed*, translated by Charles A. and Maria-Odilia Leal McBride (London: Pluto Press, 1979).

61. Claire Bishop, *Artificial Hells: Participatory Art and the Politics of Spectatorship* (New York: Verso Books, 2012), 11.

62. See Jen Harvie, *Fair Play: Art, Performance and Neoliberalism* (New York: Palgrave Macmillan, 2013). On (dance) performance's paradoxical condition as both enforced and subversive behavior, see André Lepecki, *Singularities: Dance in the Age of Performance* (New York: Routledge, 2016).

63. José Esteban Muñoz, *Cruising Utopia: The Then and There of Queer Futurity* (New York: New York University Press, 2009), 67.

64. Signed by "Subcomandante Insurgente Galeano," Marcos's speech appears in English translation in *Enlace Zapatista* as "Between Light and Shadow," http://enlacezapatista.ezln.org.mx/2014/05/27/between-light-and-shadow/.

65. For a theorization of the relationship between means and ends that engages with the concept of gesture defining it as "pure and endless mediality," see Giorgio Agamben, *Means without End: Notes on Politics*, translated by Vincenzo Binetti and Cesare Casarino (Minneapolis: University of Minnesota Press, 2000).

66. For an elaboration of the concept of "politics-as-is," see chapter 1 of Maurya Wickstrom's *Performance in the Blockades of Neoliberalism: Thinking the Political Anew* (Basingstoke: Palgrave Macmillan, 2012).

CHAPTER TWO

1. In tandem with a cacerolazo organized to repudiate the World Economic Forum at its annual meeting in New York City, activists issued a "Call for a Cacerolazo Global." The call invited activists to stage a global protest modeled on the South American cacerolazos, citing the phrase "Out with them all," the slogan used in the neighborhood assemblies in Argentina after the 2001 economic crisis. See https://www.nadir.org/nadir/initiativ/agp/free/cacerolazo/cacerolazoglobal.htm.

2. Sitrin, who was an active participant in the Occupy Wall Street movement in New York, used the term "movement of movements" in tune with characterizations of the alter-globalization movement as a "network of networks." Sitrin explains that the Argentine movement of movements followed political philosophies of self-government and horizontalism, epitomized in popular assemblies and worker-run factories. Sitrin qtd. in Jean Graham-Jones, "Rethinking Buenos Aires Theatre in the Wake of 2001 and Emerging Structures of Resistance and Resilience," *Theatre Journal* 66.1 (2014): 38.

3. The World Social Forum (WSF) is a meeting of antiglobalization organizers and civil society organizations founded in 2001. The forum's annual meetings generally match the capitalist summits of institutions such as the World Trade Organization. Under the motto "Another world is possible," the WSF contributed to the growth and momentum of the alter-globalization movement. Even though, like the Zapatistas, the WSF does not embrace a path to hegemonic power or even a unified agenda, the Forum has been crucial in stalling the development of new world orders and setting limits to greedy loan programs advanced by the IMF. See John Hammond, "The World Social Forum and the Emergence of Global Grassroots Politics," *New Politics* 11.2, whole number 42 (Winter 2007), https://newpol.org/issue_post/world-social-forum-and-emergence-global-grassroots-politics/

4. For an analysis of the relationship between digitality and social orders, see Tara McPherson, "U.S. Operating Systems at Mid-century: The Intertwining of Race and UNIX," in *Race after the Internet*, edited by Lisa Nakamura and Peter A. Chow-White (London: Routledge, 2012), 21–37.

5. Eduardo Levy Yeyati and Diego Valenzuela state that on November 30, 2001, alone US$1,164 million were relocated abroad. See *La resurrección: Historia de la poscrisis Argentina* (Buenos Aires: Editorial Sudamericana, 2007).

6. "Esta puede ser una economía soviética por 90 días para poder tener una economía norteamericana por 30 años. . . . En todos los países del mundo la movilización de dinero bancario se hace con tarjeta de débito, o de crédito, o con cheques o con transferencias financieras y el dinero en efectivo solamente se retira para el cambio chico." Domingo Cavallo, interviewed by Sergio Moreno and Maximiliano Montenegro, *Página 12*, December 2, 2001.

7. After the cacerolazos and the popular uprisings of December 19 and 20, 2001, the Argentine people continued in a state of deliberation, gathering in squares and on the streets. Institutional order took some time to be restored: in a period of ten days, five provisional presidents rotated in and out of power. Finally, in April 2003 Néstor Kirchner was elected president by regular suffrage.

8. Between December 19, 2001, and March 31, 2002, 2,014 pots-and-pans demonstrations took place in Argentina. See Claudia Briones and Marcela Mendoza, *Urban Middle-Class Women's Responses to Political Crisis in Buenos Aires* (Memphis: University of Memphis Center for Research on Women, 2001).

9. I credit sociologist Horacio González for this idea. In an interview with writer and critic María Moreno, González states: "To fill the Plaza de Mayo at 2 o'clock in the morning is one of the most violent effects of Argentine political history. It cannot not be violent. Now, I insist: how could it end? Because there was no one to represent the state. There was no state. The state was an empty symbol, a gas. I thought it was fascinating because I had the experience in mind of that almost unconscious moment in national history when someone always comes out onto the balcony. And because there was no possibility that anyone would come out onto the balcony, it had to finish as it did: with tear gas, panic, shots." Published originally as "Cacerolas, multitud, pueblo," *Página 12*, February 11, 2002. Available in English in the *Journal of Latin American Cultural Studies* 11.2 (2002).

10. *Argentinazo* is the name mainstream media used to refer to the popular rebellion to highlight the volatile climate the country was undergoing and the courageous popular response to it.

11. Although in a context of increased criminalization of protest and media vilification of collective dissent the use of the cross to signal nonviolence and ethics may seem appropriate, this image is haunted by the many instances of religious violence that belong to the history of the Americas as a continent in which colonization was promoted as part of a religious crusade.

12. In his bodily defiance of overpowering repression, the picture of the man with the cross resonates with a mythical image of a twentieth-century protest: the "tank man," the man who, nonchalantly, carrying what appears to be grocery shopping bags, stood in front of a line of military tanks in Tiananmen Square during the 1989 pro-democracy student protests. I am grateful to dance scholar André Lepecki for this association.

13. Eduardo Basualdo, *Sistema político y modelo de acumulación en la Argentina: Notas sobre el transformismo argentino durante la valorización finaciera (1976–2001)* (Buenos Aires: Universidad Nacional de Quilmes Ediciones, 2001).

14. Gilpin qtd. in Malcolm Waters, *Globalization* (London: Routledge, 2001), 50.

15. Ibid., 51, 105.

16. Since 1944, the World Bank and the International Monetary Fund have set policy prescriptions for debt-ridden nations soliciting financial support. These specific reforms imposed by these institutions as conditions for loan disbursements compromise the indebted countries' sovereignty and self-determination. John Williamson's 1989 "Washington Consensus" summarizes

the IMF's and the World Bank's prescriptions as a list of ten reform "command-ments" promoted by Washington-based institutions.

17. Naúm Minsburg, ed., *Los guardianes del dinero: Las políticas del FMI en Argentina* (Buenos Aires: Grupo Editorial Norma, 2003).

18. This system of financial transfers favorable to a selected group of local and international investors was called the "financial bicycle" to illustrate the "self-breeding" logics of speculation. As in the image of a fixed bicycle that re-flects movement *in itself*, not movement *toward*, in the financial bicycle capital valorization was achieved through mere money movement, that is, money qua money valorization, as opposed to the use of money in support of production or long-term infrastructure.

19. Llistar quoted in Laura Ramos, *El fracaso del Consenso de Washington: La caída de su mejor alumno, Argentina* (Barcelona: Icaria Editorial, 2003).

20. Javier Auyero, *La protesta: Relatos de la beligerancia popular en la Argentina democrática* (Buenos Aires: Libros del Rojas, 2002).

21. On the origins of the *piquetero* movement narrated by women protago-nists, see *Piqueteras*, a documentary directed by Malena Bystrowicz and Verónica Mastrosimone, https://www.youtube.com/watch?v=TMSj0J9ktuI.

22. See Colectivo Situaciones, *19 y 20: Apuntes para el nuevo protagonismo so-cial* (Buenos Aires: Ediciones de Mano en Mano, 2002), 150. Available in English as *19 & 20: Notes for a New Social Protagonism*, translated by Nate Holdren and Sebastian Touza (New York: Minor Compositions, 2011).

23. See Marina Sitrin, "One No, Many Yeses," in *Occupy! Scenes from Occu-pied America,* edited by Astra Taylor et al. (London: Verso, 2011), 7–11.

24. "Promo del día: deposite dólares y le devolvemos mierda."

25. TPS was created as part of a neighborhood assembly, modeled on the Mexican Talleres de Gráfica Popular (People's Print Workshop), a 1930s project that approached art-making as a tool for supporting the struggle of workers in postrevolutionary Mexico. In turn, GAC contributed visual tactics to the *es-craches* organized by H.I.J.O.S., an organization created by the children of the disappeared in the mid-1990s. As part of this organization's acts of denuncia-tion of those involved in acts of kidnapping and/or torture during the military dictatorship, GAC created and installed urban markers simulating traffic signs to disclose the locations of the houses of military personnel living in impunity as well as clandestine detention centers.

26. Mabel Bellucci and Karina Granieri, "En Brukman se cosen las redes so-ciales," *Página 12*, November 10, 2003, https://www.pagina12.com.ar/diario/suplementos/las12/13-853-2003-11-10.html

27. For critical genealogies of socially engaged art see Claire Bishop, *Artifi-cial Hells: Participatory Art and the Politics of Spectatorship* (New York: Verso Books, 2012); and Jen Harvie, *Fair Play: Art, Performance and Neoliberalism* (New York: Palgrave Macmillan, 2013).

28. Andrea Giunta, *Poscrisis: Arte argentino después de 2001* (Buenos Aires: Si-glo Veintiuno Editores, 2009), 66.

29. Graham-Jones, "Rethinking Buenos Aires Theatre."

30. See Naomi Klein, "Farewell to 'The End of History': Organisation and Vision in Anti-corporate Movements," *Socialist Register*, March 19, 2009.

31. For the role of new media in the Seattle protests see T. V. Reed, "Will

the Revolution Be Cybercast? New Media, the Battle of Seattle, and Global Justice," in *The Art of Protest: Culture and Activism from the Civil Rights Movement to the Streets of Seattle* (Minneapolis: University of Minnesota Press, 2005).

32. On Indymedia as a community of resistance to the enclosure or privatization of the internet, see Dorothy Kidd, "Indymedia.org: A New Communications Commons," in *Cyberactivism: Online Activism in Theory and in Practice*, edited by Martha McCaughey and Michael D. Ayers (New York: Routledge, 2003), 47–69. On Indymedia as an actualization of ideals of radical democracy, see Victor Pickard, "Assessing the Radical Democracy of Indymedia: Discursive, Technical, and Institutional Constructions," *Critical Studies in Media Communication* 23.1 (2006): 19–38.

33. See Hammond, "World Social Forum."

34. Hammond, ibid., also notes that these issues are not exclusive to digital networking. He states that the alter-globalization movement was divided into two camps: the anarchists who favored direct action and disruptive tactics at corporate and trade summits, and the activists who gathered at the WSF, embraced methods of deliberative democracy, and rejected unified declarations or consensus-based organizing. There was also the branch that favored nongovernmental organizing (NGO) and policymaking, a process that some critiqued as separatist. These issues are also discussed in Sonia Alvarez et al., eds., *Beyond Civil Society: Activism, Participation and Protest in Latin America* (Durham, NC: Duke University Press, 2017).

35. This refers to the expanded power of decision-making granted to Finance Minister Cavallo during Menem's administration.

36. My translation. The Hemispheric Institute of Performance and Politics published the PowerPoint presentation in its Spring 2002 newsletter. See http://hemisphericinstitute.org/eng/newsletter/issue5/ARGENTINA2001.htm

37. The use of cooking references responds to the fact that the IMF's directives became popularly known as "cooking recipes." In one of its exhibits, in the aftermath of the 2001 *estallido*, the Museum of Debt in Buenos Aires actually included a doll kitchen called "la cocina del FMI" (the IMF's kitchen) as a prop to explain the IMF's lending conditions and their detrimental effects on the Argentine economy.

38. Note that, like street mobilization itself, cacerolazos can be used by progressive and reactionary movements alike. In fact, at the time of this writing, in Argentina cacerolazos (including, for some critics, those dating back to 2001) are cataloged by progressive sectors as a classist and reactionary protest used mainly by upper-middle-class protesters in defense of their interests. Critics use the expression *cacerolas de teflón* (signaling expensive pots and pans as a mark of privilege) to refer to the pots-and-pans protests organized by destabilizing sectors in 2008 and 2012 against President Cristina Fernández de Kirchner's interventionist policies. Conversely, in Chile, although pots-and-pans protests were used in the 1970s by right-wing protesters against Salvador Allende's socialist administration, in 2011 demonstrators banged pots and pans to show their support of the student movement that demanded public education.

39. In their essay "Producciones digitales anónimas," Jimena Durán Prieto and Esteban Javier Rico argue that by sharing digital productions such as *Ar-*

gentina2001.ppt activists sought to build trust and legitimate their claims among those not copresent in street demonstrations or assemblies. In *Piquete de Ojo: visualidades de la crisis. Argentina 2001–2003,* edited by María Ledesma and Paula Siganevich (Buenos Aires: Ediciones FADU, 2008), 83–104.

40. TheAnonMessage2, *Anonymous Operation Vocalize,* video, 2:58, posted on February 2012, https://www.youtube.com/watch?v=DjtU-iM8vlw

41. Anonymous's call for *cacerolazos* conveys the group's characteristic ironic tone while also addressing the important fact that not all people are able to join street protests and risk detention.

42. Occupy drew from the Zapatistas' horizontal democracy practices and also from the Argentine neighborhood assemblies. The online/offline connection that Anonymous makes here between Occupy and other movements focused on predatory capitalism is important and underresearched. About the use of new media in the Occupy movement, see Sasha Costanza-Chock, "Mic Check! Media Cultures and the Occupy Movement," *Social Movement Studies* 11.3–4 (August 2012): 375–385.

43. In Maria Moreno, "Interview with Horacio González," *Journal of Latin American Cultural Studies* 11.2 (2002): 145.

44. Randy Martin, "After Economy? Social Logics of the Derivative," *Social Text 144* 31.1 (2013): 89.

45. My thanks to anthropologist Diego Zenobi, who introduced me to this protest performance and to Marcelo Wakstein.

46. Levy Yeyati and Valenzuela state that, following the government's freeze of bank accounts, US$61,100 million were "trapped" in banks. See Levy Yeyati and Valenzuela, *La resurrección.*

47. Fifty-seven percent of the deposits locked by the bank freeze were accounts of less than US$50,000. See Ignaci Brunet Icart and Fernanda Laura Schilman, *Convivir con el capital financiero: Corralito y movimientos ahorristas (Argentina 2001–2004)* (Caracas: Editorial Fundamentos, 2005).

48. *Escraches* are site-specific acts of popular justice carried out by the human rights organization H.I.J.O.S. *Escraches* repudiated the amnesty granted to the military by the democratic governments of Raúl Alfonsin and Carlos Menem. In their *escraches* H.I.J.O.S disclose the location of the homes of military personnel, economists, physicians, and others accused of being involved in the kidnapping, torture, and disappearance of their parents during the Argentine "Dirty War."

49. Diego Zenobi, "Protesta social, violencia y performances: Narraciones de *orden* y prácticas de *desorden* en las marchas de los 'ahorristas estafados,'" master's thesis, Universidad de Buenos Aires, 2004.

50. Marcelo Wakstein, personal interview with the author, Buenos Aires, Argentina, September 27, 2005.

51. Ibid.

52. See Larry Elliot, "Do Cry for Us," *The Guardian,* June 6, 2002; and Sophie Arie, "Plumber's 'Bank Holiday' Protest at Saving Freeze," *The Telegraph,* January 26, 2002.

53. Rorberto Roglich (age sixty-two), who entered a bank with a grenade in January 2002, and Norma Albino (age fifty-nine), who set herself on fire in May

2002, are perhaps the most extreme responses to the *corralito* decree, which ended on December 2, 2002.

54. Daniel Schiller, *Digital Capitalism: Networking the Global Market System* (Cambridge, MA: MIT Press, 1999).

55. Ignacio Lewkowicz, *Sucesos Argentinos: Cacerolazo y subjetividad postestatal* (Buenos Aires: Paidós, 2003).

56. Levy Yeyati and Valenzuela, *La resurrección*.

57. See Claudio Scaletta, "Los bancos actuaron como autopistas para la fuga," *Página 12*, October 22, 2003.

58. Martin, "After Economy."

59. In January 2012, Occupy Oakland launched the action "Move-in Day," calling protesters to occupy a vacant building, the Henry J. Kaiser Convention Center. This action was unsuccessful and ended in hundreds of arrests.

60. Wakstein estimates that 1.5 million people were affected by this decree. The government offered bank account holders several options to recover their devaluated money, most of which involved bonds and other deferred solutions.

61. Wakstein, interview with the author.

62. "El banco está hecho para ganar plata. Si vos no le permitís trabajar, el banco pierde plata. Bueno, la idea nuestra era esa: no permitirle trabajar al banco. Es decir, nosotros no podíamos trabajar porque teníamos que estar protestando. Bueno, era devolverle con la misma moneda al banco, dentro de los medios que nosotros podíamos."

63. Elizabeth Jelin, ed., *Women and Social Change in Latin America* (London: Zed Books, 1990), 5.

64. See Moreno, "Interview with Nicolás Casullo," 151–156; and Sebastián Carassai, "The Noisy Majority: An Analysis of the Argentine Crisis of December 2001 from the Theoretical Approach of Hardt & Negri, Laclau and Žižek," *Journal of Latin American Cultural Studies* 16.1 (2007): 45–62.

65. For a transcription of Alcaraz's speech in Congress, see "No somos ni vamos a ser criadas," *Cosecha Roja*, May 29, 2018, http://cosecharoja.org/florencia-alcaraz-no-somos-ni-vamos-ser-criadas/

66. See Graciela Di Marco, "Social Movement Demands in Argentina and the Constitution of 'A Feminist People,'" in Alvarez et al., *Beyond Civil Society*, 122-140.

67. This is in reference to the 354 workers (journalists and photographers) from the state-run media agency Telam who were laid off in late June 2018 and reinstated by a judicial order in mid-July. Activists celebrated the news on Facebook, stating, "Luchar sirve" (To struggle is worthwhile).

CHAPTER THREE

1. The idea was suggested by public policy student Felipe Villaseca Vega on Facebook on June 15, 2011.

2. Following Bahktin, I define the eventness of performance as the affective force of an experience that carries emotion, volition, and value beyond its orig-

inal execution, driving spectators to continue interacting with it, as we will see in this chapter. See Peter Wright and John McCarthy, *Technology as Experience* (Cambridge, MA: MIT Press, 2004), 76.

3. Flash mobs, or smart mobs, are ephemeral, often highly stylized occupations of physical space by hastily assembled crowds. In flash mobs, unacquainted people perform as an "intelligent mass," swarming a space to quickly dissipate after the convened action is over. See Howard Rheingold, *Smart Mobs: The Next Social Revolution* (Cambridge: Basic Books, 2002), xii.

4. Performance artist and scholar María José Contreras Lorenzini shows that in the 1990s in Chile the discourse of the free market promoted ideas of freedom that confused individual liberty with civil rights. Citizens who had been repressed during Pinochet's dictatorship then transitioned smoothly to docile democratic participation, becoming precarious subjects whose only agency was to acquire goods and services. See "A Woman Artist in the Neoliberal Chilean Jungle," in *Performance, Feminism and Affect in Neoliberal Times*, edited by Elin Diamond, Denise Varney and Candice Amich (London: Palgrave Macmillan, 2017), 239–251.

5. Sebastián Valenzuela et al., "The Social Media Basis of Youth Protest Behavior: The Case of Chile," *Journal of Communication* 62.2 (2012): 299–314.

6. "Las siete modernizaciones," *Memoria Chilena*, Biblioteca Nacional de Chile, http://www.memoriachilena.cl/602/w3-article-93006.html.

7. Ibid.

8. Giorgio Jackson and Camila Vallejo, "Gato por liebre," *The Clinic Online*, July 14, 2011, http://www.theclinic.cl/2011/07/14/gato-por-liebre/

9. Ibid.

10. Cummings notes that the increased access to education reached by 2011 (seven out of ten university students were first-generation) created a false sense of mobility, locking families in long-term loan repayment plans. Peter M. M. Cummings, "Student Movement in Chile: Explaining a Protest Paradox," *Panoramas: Scholarly Platform*, February 21, 2017, http://www.panoramas.pitt.edu/health-and-society/student-movement-chile-explaining-protest-paradox

11. Cristian Cabalin, "Neoliberal Education and Student Movements in Chile: Inequalities and Malaise," *Policy Futures in Education* 10.2 (2012): 219–228.

12. Maurizio Lazzarato, *The Making of the Indebted Man: An Essay on the Neoliberal Condition*, translated by Joshua David Jordan (Los Angeles: Semiotext(e), 2012).

13. Ibid.

14. Franco "Bifo" Berardi, "Cognitarian Subjectivation," *e-flux* 20 (2010), http://www.e-flux.com/journal/cognitarian-subjectivation/

15. Harney and Moten define debt governance poetically: "The student has no interests. The student's interests must be identified, declared, pursued, assessed, counseled, and credited. Debt produces interests. The student will be indebted. The student will be interested. Interest the students! The student can be calculated by her debts, can calculate her debts with her interests. She is in sight of credit, in sight of graduation, in sight of being a creditor, of being in-

vested in education, a citizen." See Stefano Harney and Fred Moten, *The Under-commons: Fugitive Planning and Black Study* (New York: Minor Compositions, 2013), 67.

16. Lazzarato, *Making of the Indebted Man*.

17. Ibid.

18. Ibid., 8.

19. Ibid.

20. The 2006 cycle of student protests was called the "Penguin Revolution" because of the black-and-white uniforms worn by high school students in Chile. From April to early June, students sustained nationwide mobilizations demanding sweeping changes in an educational system that they saw was consolidating socioeconomic inequality. Years later, some of these protesters became active members of the 2011 demonstrations as university students.

21. CONFECH is the acronym for Confederación de Estudiantes de Chile (Chilean Students' Confederation). Its leaders are elected democratically without intervention from university administrators. CONFECH's leaders, Camila Vallejo and Giorgio Jackson, became internationally known during the student protests of 2011. In 2013, they gained seats in the chamber of deputies under the administration of President Michelle Bachelet.

22. The website *Cartografía de la movilización estudiantil* maps out more than a thousand protest actions and their corresponding press coverage. http://www.cartografiadelamovilizacion.cl/.

23. Cummings argues that the students' collective identification helped them overcome the political disaffection undergone by their parents and grand-parents due to their traumatic past. He contends that generational life experiences are a catalyzer for political action that can influence collective insurgent identities. See Cummings, "Student Movement in Chile."

24. Diamela Eltit, interview by Diana Taylor, in *What Is Performance Studies?*, edited by Diana Taylor and Marcos Steuernagel (Durham, NC: Duke University Press; New York: HemiPress, 2015), http://scalar.usc.edu/nehvectors/wips/diamela-eltit-english

25. Nelly Richard, *Margins and Institutions: Art in Chile since 1973* (Melbourne: Art and Text, 1986), 21.

26. The call was originally published in the no longer available *Thriller por la educación* Facebook event page. https://es-es.facebook.com/events/241260249219635/

27. Paolo Gerbaudo, *Tweets and the Streets: Social Media and Contemporary Activism* (London: Pluto; New York: Palgrave Macmillan, 2012).

28. aurits1985, *Maquillaje Zombie Thriller x la Educación Shile*, June 23, 2011, https://www.youtube.com/watch?v=0WwTQUQqqdk

29. Gerbaudo, *Tweets and the Streets*.

30. Jason Farman, *Mobile Interface Theory: Embodied Space and Locative Media* (London: Routledge, 2012).

31. Raúl Sánchez Cedillo and other theorists of networked social movements use the concept of stigmergy (*estigmergia*), borrowed from insect biology, to explain what they call "distributed democracy." Focusing on the 2011 Spanish Revolution, these theorists analyze how agents who were separated in time and

space were able to act in concert without having to delay decision-making to moments of copresence. See Raúl Sánchez Cedillo, "El 15 M como insurrección del cuerpo máquina," in *Democracia distribuida: Miradas de la Universidad Nómada al 15M*, Universidad Nómada, 2012, 49–65.

32. In a manner that resonates with my concept of performance constellations as a logic of relation and sustained eventness, Seigworth and Gregg define affect as "an impingement or extrusion of a momentary or sometimes more sustained state of relation *as well as the passage* (and the duration of passage) of forces of intensities." See Melissa Gregg and Gregory J. Seigworth, eds., *The Affect Theory Reader* (Durham, NC: Duke University Press, 2010), 1.

33. See danah boyd, "Participating in the Always-On Lifestyle," in *The Social Media Reader*, edited by Michael Mandiberg (New York: New York University Press, 2012), 71–76.

34. The "zombie" is a canonical horror movie figure appropriated by the West from Haitian folklore. Born from the "complex colonial history of the Americas," in contemporary protests zombies came to represent "the slave, a silent worker whose humanity has been consumed and whose existence is living death." See Sherry R. Truffin, "Zombies in the Classroom: Education as Consumption in Two Novels by Joyce Carol Oates," in *Zombies in the Academy: Living Death in Higher Education*, edited by Andrew Whelan, Ruth Walker, and Christopher Moore (Chicago: University of Chicago Press, 2013), 207.

35. Judith Hamera, "The Labors of Michael Jackson: Virtuosity, Deindustrialization, and Dancing Work," *PMLA* 127.4 (2012): 751–765.

36. Ibid., 755.

37. Zygmunt Bauman, *Liquid Modernity* (Cambridge, MA: Polity Press, 2000).

38. On permanent training as one of the main mechanisms of societies of control, see Gilles Deleuze, "Postscript on the Societies of Control," *October* 59 (1992): 3–7. See also Alessandro Fornazzari, *Speculative Fictions: Chilean Culture, Economics, and the Neoliberal Transition* (Pittsburgh: University of Pittsburgh Press, 2013).

39. See Christian Marazzi, *Capital and Language: From the New Economy to the War Economy*, translated by Gregory Conti (Los Angeles: Semiotext(e), 2008).

40. See Rebecca Schneider, "It Seems as If . . . I Am Dead: Zombie Capitalism and Theatrical Labor," *TDR: The Drama Review* 56.4 (2012): 150–162.

41. On networked free labor, see Tiziana Terranova, *Network Culture: Politics for the Information Age* (London: Pluto Press, 2004); and Berardi, "Cognitarian Subjectivation."

42. waiwenkref pirilongko, *Thriller masivo por la educación chilena (Basta de jilessss)*, video, 8:26, June 24, 2011, https://www.youtube.com/watch?v=tR12Vi6BvrI

43. Fábio Malini and Henrique Antoun, *@Internet e #rua: Ciberativismo e mobilização nas redes sociais* (Porto Alegre: Sulina, 2013), 211.

44. To define the ontology of performance as a nonreproductive event, Peggy Phelan famously claimed that "performance's only life is in the present." See *Unmarked: The Politics of Performance* (London: Routledge, 1993), 146.

45. Diana Taylor, "Save as . . . Knowledge and Transmission in the Age of

Digital Technologies," *Imagining America,* 2010, Paper 7, http://surface.syr.edu/ia/7.

46. I expand on this issue in chapter 4 by engaging with Wendy Hui Kyong Chun's concept of enduring ephemerality, from which Taylor builds her characterization of digital memory.

47. Philip Auslander, "Digital Liveness: A Historico-Philosophical Perspective," *PAJ: A Journal of Performance and Art* 34.3 (2012): 3–11.

48. Analyzing the web as a temporal medium, Weltevrede et al. argue that the Web 2.0 promotes real-time as a feature that differentiates the participatory web from the previous, still in play, one-to-many network of web pages and links. These authors claim that in the Web 2.0, real-time is not immediacy but speed, or rather, pace. Real-time is made out of different paces that respond to the user's drive toward freshness and relevance, which are the main forms of organizing content online today. Esther Weltevrede et al., "The Politics of Real-Time: A Device Perspective on Social Media Platforms and Search Engines," *Theory, Culture & Society* (2014): 1–26.

49. Edison Cájas, *1800 horas por la educación,* video, 4:26, August 7, 2011, https://vimeo.com/27418149

50. Sergio Gilabert, personal interview with the author, May 21, 2013.

51. "¡Corre! 1800 horas por la educación. Alrededor de la Moneda desde el 13 de junio al 26 de agosto ¡yo me muevo por la educación gratuita. Ven y únete." 1800 horas por la Educación, Facebook.com, June 13, 2011. My translation.

52. A central prop in the street version of the performance that exemplifies the synergy between on- and offline participation was a sign displaying the hours covered by runners toward the *1,800 Hours* goal. This sign served to mark milestones that would be displayed on site and celebrated through pictures online.

53. Alain Badiou, *Theoretical Writings,* edited and translated by Ray Brassier and Alberto Toscano (London: Continuum, 2004), 153.

54. In the street protest, a black flag carrying the legend "Free Education Now" served as the baton that was passed from one group or participant to another, helping to identify the cause.

55. There are two documentaries that feature the eighteen-hundred-hour run: *El vals de los inútiles* (The waltz of the useless) by Edison Cájas (2013) and *Ya no basta con marchar* (Demonstrating is no longer enough) by Hernán Saavedra (2016). Sergio Gilabert, the student who suggested the idea of running during eighteen hundred hours, created a documentary theater piece called *El año internacional del olvido* (The international year of oblivion) (2016), in which performers return to the experience of the run as a way of reminding spectators that the issue continues unresolved and that the fight for public education should go on.

56. As I explain in the introduction, protests in Latin America have energized political processes, providing spaces for citizens to create and recreate themselves politically. However, states are not always willing to process what people in the streets demand back into institutional channels, and this is why states increasingly repress popular collective assembly. In this context, the stu-

dents' creativity to enliven modes of political participation that are perceived as quaint, such as demonstrations, recognizes the value of public, collective mobilization while acknowledging that it needs to be updated. Still, categories such as "students," "citizens," and "workers" are important signifiers of political positions vis-à-vis the state.

57. Gilabert, interview.

58. Ibid.

59. Zizi Papacharissi, *Affective Publics: Sentiment, Technology, and Politics* (Oxford: Oxford University Press, 2014), 126.

60. Malini and Antoun, *@Internet e #rua*, 245.

61. Ibid., 246.

62. "Cómo querés que te lo diga? Bailando? Haciendo de zombie? Corriendo?" Gilabert, interview.

63. "En 1800 Horas el gobierno no se movió por la educación," *The Clinic Online*, August 27, 2011, http://www.theclinic.cl/2011/08/27/en-1800-horas-gobierno-no-se-movio-por-la-educacion/

64. Lazzarato, *Making of the Indebted Man*, 41.

65. Jacques Rancière, *The Politics of Aesthetics: The Distribution of the Sensible*, translated by Gabriel Rockhill (London: Continuum, 2006).

CHAPTER FOUR

1. Michelle Zappavigna, "Ambient Affiliation: A Linguistic Perspective on Twitter," *New Media & Society* 13.5 (2011): 788–806.

2. Sanjay Sharma, "Black Twitter? Racial Hashtags, Networks and Contagion," *New Formations* 78 (Summer 2012): 46.

3. See José Van Dijck, *The Culture of Connectivity: A Critical History of Social Media* (Oxford: Oxford University Press, 2013), 71–72.

4. Jeff Scheible, *Digital Shift: The Cultural Logic of Punctuation* (Minneapolis: University of Minnesota Press, 2015).

5. Yarimar Bonilla and Jonathan Rosa, "#Ferguson: Digital Protest, Hashtag Ethnography, and the Racial Politics of Social Media in the United States," *American Anthropologist* 119 (March 2017): 5.

6. In contrast to Zappavigna's theory of affiliation via searching, Bonilla and Rosa (ibid.) caution against a unidirectional approach to hashtags and give examples of #Ferguson as an anchor of activism for black lives as well as racist countermobilization. These examples show how "Search for me and affiliate with my values" can go in several directions, no matter how defined the hashtag is.

7. Bonilla and Rosa state that movements such as Black Lives Matter not only underscore the value of black lives vis-à-vis police brutality but also provide concrete ways in which social media can become a site for reevaluating "black materiality." With this they mean that social media become a site for contesting the meanings associated with black bodies, particularly black youth, as they are depicted in mainstream media under victim-blaming, stigmatizing narratives. See ibid., 154–156.

8. Ni Una Menos (Not One Woman Less) is a feminist Argentine collective dedicated to fight gender-based violence. The collective, integrated by journalists, writers, attorneys, academics, activists, and artists, formed in March 2015 in response to the proliferation of cases of femicide and ensuing toxic media coverage. Black Lives Matter is a US racial justice movement founded by activists Alicia Garza, Patrisse Cullors, and Opal Tometi. These activists created the hashtag #BlackLivesMatter in July 2013, following George Zimmerman's acquittal after murdering Trayvon Martin, a seventeen-year-old African American teen. Deen Freelon, Charlton D. Mcilwain, and Meredith D. Clark claim that #BlackLivesMatter came to "signify a movement" starting in August 2014, during the #Ferguson protests that followed the murder of Mike Brown, an eighteen-year-old African American recent high school graduate, shot by officer Darren Wilson on August 9. Freelon et al. state that #BlackLivesMatter went from being included in forty-eight public tweets in June 2014 to 52,288 by August 2014. After the Ferguson protests Garza, Cullors, and Tometi founded Black Lives Matter as a chapter-based activist organization. See Deen Freelon, Charlton D. Mcilwain, and Meredith D. Clark, "Beyond the Hashtags: #Ferguson, #BlackLivesMatter, and the Online Struggle for Offline Justice," research report, Center for Media & Social Impact, 2016.

9. For an excellent analysis of Black Lives Matter as a networked movement, see ibid.

10. Problematizing the issue of "presence," that is, the "here and now" defining feature of performance, Heathfield claims that "the varied deployments of altered time in contemporary performance invariably bring the artwork towards the condition of eventhood. . . . This condition is often decidedly unstable and ambivalent, for whilst the artist's or the spectator's 'presence' in the moment may be a pre-requisite, the transient and elusive nature of this presence becomes the subject of the work. You really had to be there, as the saying goes. But often 'being there,' in the heart of things, you are reminded of the impossibility of ever being fully present to oneself, to others or to the artwork. Eventhood allows spectators to live for a while in the paradox of two impossible desires: to be present in the moment, to savor it, and to save the moment, to still and preserve its power long after it's gone." Adrian Heathfield, *Live: Art and Performance* (London: Tate, 2004), 9.

11. *Time*, February 24, 2014.

12. A meme is "a unit of cultural transmission" that replicates like genes. The term was coined by evolutionary biologist Richard Dawkins in his 1976 book *The Selfish Gene* to understand how ideas spread and how cultural change happens. Dawkins created the term "meme" from the Greek word *mimesthai*, meaning "to imitate." See Patrick Reinsborough and Doyle Canning, "Memes," in *Beautiful Trouble*, edited by Andrew Boyd and Dave Oswald Mitchell (New York: OR Books, 2012), 242–243.

13. Van Dijck, *The Culture of Connectivity*.

14. In his analysis of racialized humor and "blacktags" in what is known as "Black Twitter," Sanjay Sharma defines popular hashtags or memes as "media-friendly monikers" that encapsulate the mood of the moment. See Sharma, "Black Twitter," 48.

15. Richard Roman and Edur Velasco Arregui, "The Specter of Ayotzinapa Haunts the Continent," *NACLA Reporting On the Americas*, December 8, 2014, https://nacla.org/news/2014/12/07/spectre-ayotzinapa-haunts-continent

16. For an account of so-called Peña bots and general uses of bots as "automated propaganda," see Erin Gallagher's *Medium* compilation, "México: Articles about Bots and Trolls," January 1, 2017, https://medium.com/@erin_gallagher/news-articles-about-bots-trolls-in-mexican-networks-7b1e551ef4a6

17. For a succinct explanation of uses of *détournement* / culture jamming in contemporary activisms, see Boyd and Mitchell, *Beautiful Trouble*, 28–29.

18. The Escuelas Normales Rurales, or Rural Teachers' Schools, is a school system founded in the early 1920s after the Mexican Revolution of 1910–1920. These schools' main goal was to provide reading and writing instruction as well as farming techniques to create conditions for impoverished, illiterate communities to become autonomous. Because state funds for these schools have been drastically diminished as part of the general dismantling of public education in Mexico, these institutions are supported by teachers' unions and other regional groups. See Roberto Arteaga and Francisco Muciño, "La historia no contada de Ayotzinapa y las Normales Rurales," *Forbes Mexico*, December 25, 2014, http://www.forbes.com.mx/la-historia-no-contada-de-ayotzinapa-y-las-normales-rurales/

19. In turn, three years after Ayotzinapa, Argentinian protesters appropriated the statement "We want them alive" (Vivos los queremos) and used "We want him alive" (Vivo lo queremos) in the case of the disappearance of Santiago Maldonado, a twenty-seven-year-old man who went missing on August 1, 2017, while he participated in a protest by the Mapuche people as part of their land and human rights struggles in Patagonia.

20. For an excellent analysis of the circulation of the Ayotzinapa students' pictures, see Rossana Reguillo, "Rostros en escenas: La imposibilidad del desentendimiento," *Magis* (ITESO), December 1, 2014, https://magis.iteso.mx/content/rostros-en-escenas-ayotzinapa-y-la-imposibilidad-del-desentendimiento

21. Reguillo uses "narco-machine" to define the particular forms of violence enacted by narco traffickers in order to exhibit their symbolic power. Reguillo analyzes massive graves and the particular dehumanizing stagings of bodies as registers of the phantasmagoric presence of narco power that exercises structural, historical, disciplining, and diffuse violence. Rossana Reguillo, "The Narco-Machine and the Work of Violence: Notes toward Its Identification," *e-misférica* 8.2, http://hemisphericinstitute.org/hemi/en/e-misferica-82/reguillo.

22. See, for example, the teach-in "When Governments Kill Their Students" organized by the Hemispheric Institute of Performance and Politics in New York City. https://vimeo.com/114715184.

23. Octavio Guerra explains how the war on drugs launched by president Felipe Calderón in 2006 "has served a policy of class war and social control" epitomized by counterinsurgency tactics and the presence of military forces in urban settings for over a decade. Guerra defines the Ayotzinapa students' case as "emblematic of the despotism of an elite accustomed to impunity and an exemplary punishment with a clear political agenda." See Octavio Guerra,

"The Open Veins of Mexico: Three Years after Ayotzinapa," in *Until We Find You: The Disappeared of Ayotzinapa* (New York: HemiPress, 2017). http://untilwe-findyou.tome.press/chapter/the-open-veins-of-mexico/.

24. Ayotzinapa became a turning point, sparked and supported by social media mobilization on the heels of the 2012 student movement #YoSoy132 that defied Peña Nieto during his presidential campaign and beyond.

25. Rossana Reguillo, *Paisajes insurrectos: Jóvenes, redes y revueltas en el otoño civilizatorio* (NED Ediciones, 2017). Kindle.

26. Silvia Tabachnik, "La construcción del acontecimiento en la era de Internet," *Mediaciones de la Comunicación* 11 (2016): 182.

27. Scheible, *Digital Shift*.

28. In fact, in April 14, 2010, the Library of Congress announced that Twitter had given it the archive of all public tweets posted between 2006 and 2010. From that day, the library began to archive these cultural artifacts, even though this repository has not been yet made accessible to the public. As of January 1, 2018, the library collects only a select pool of tweets. It is important to remember that, even though tweets are brief forms of textual communication, they contain a wealth of metadata, such as information about their creator (information that is actually mined by companies for marketing and product-placement purposes), making the 140-character message a much more extensive document.

29. Senator Bernie Sanders marked a high point in the history of current-day Twitter-motorized politics when he included an oversized printout of a 2015 tweet by Donald J. Trump as part of one of his presentations during the early 2017 Affordable Care Act debate. What is interesting about this example (and about the way tweets are cited in newscasts) is that tweets perform as visual referents that include much more than the quoted text. The image of the tweet that includes the name, picture, and user account or handle of the addresser evokes the presence of that person in a digitally mediated forum. Visually cited in decision-making or newscast spaces, tweets pull audiences into the affective atmosphere of social media platforms, restoring the emotional feel of the statement in an offline, albeit digitally driven, here and now.

30. Toret differentiates technopolitics from clicktivism and cyberactivism, arguing that, in contrast to digital activism, technopolitical mobilization generates a multilayered system that links physical/urban space, mass-media space, and digital networks, or what he calls "transmedia space." Javier Toret et al., "Tecnopolítica: La potencia de las multitudes conectadas: El sistema red 15M, un nuevo paradigma de la política distribuida," Internet Disciplinary Institute, IN3 Working Paper Series RR-13-001, June 18, 2013, http://tecnopolitica.net/sites/default/files/1878-5799-3-PB%20%282%29.pdf

31. Note how both Black Lives Matter and Ni Una Menos emerged as indignant responses to the proliferation of killings of black people in the United States and of women, lesbians, *travetis*, trans and nonbinaries (as per the movement's established terms), and both quickly became sustained social movements drawing attention to institutionalized, systemic racial and gendered violence.

32. Bonilla and Rosa, "#Ferguson."

33. Wendy Hui Kyong Chun, "The Enduring Ephemeral, or the Future Is a Memory," *Critical Inquiry* 35.1 (2008): 149.

34. See Andrea Gompf, "Was the #YaMeCansé Hashtag Hijacked by EPN Twitter Bots?," *Remezcla*, December 5, 2014. http://remezcla.com/culture/was-yamecanse-hashtag-hijacked-by-epn-bots/

35. On digitally mediated censorship, see Emiliano Treré, "The Dark Side of Digital Politics: Understanding the Algorithmic Manufacturing of Consent and the Hindering of Online Dissidence," *IDS Bulletin* 47.1 (January 24, 2016), http://bulletin.ids.ac.uk/idsbo/article/view/41

36. Bots are computer programs that automate behaviors such as tweeting, following, and liking. Bot spam attacks affect legitimate trending hashtags, causing Twitter's algorithm to shut down these hashtags under suspicion of bogus activity. See Gompf, "#YaMeCansé Hashtag."

37. Guerra, "Open Veins of Mexico."

38. Eric Garner, a forty-three-year-old African American man, was killed by a chokehold performed by Officer Daniel Pantaleo on July 17, 2014, in Staten Island. A witness recorded the incident. Garner's words "I can't breathe" became a poignant, viral event that triggered heated responses on social media.

39. Witness accounts that Brown had raised his hands in surrender at the time he was shot sparked outrage and inspired the hashtag #HandsUpDont-Shoot to underscore police brutality and the precarious conditions of black lives under systemic racism.

40. Social media cultural forms such as #Fergusinapa constitute effective acts of solidarity and resistance in response to transnational systems that demonstrate the force of coloniality in contemporary times. Anibal Quijano terms the persistence of colonial power in contemporary times "coloniality of power." Located as the other side of modernity, coloniality of power denounces modernity as a social fiction that necessitated the institution of racial difference as a basis for controlling resources and labor. See Aníbal Quijano, "Coloniality of Power, Eurocentrism, and Latin America," *Nepantla: Views from South* 1.3 (2000): 533–581.

41. Van Dijck, *The Culture of Connectivity*, 88.

42. "Distributed democracy" refers to the counterpower network that emerged in response to financial crisis and the crisis of democratic systems. See *Democracia distribuida: Miradas de la Universidad Nómada al 15M*," Universidad Nómada, 2012, http://www.trasversales.net/ddun15m.pdf.

43. The election of leftist candidate Manuel López Obrador in 2018, and the discourses that accompanied his triumph emphasizing civic engagement in a context of democratic revitalization, are undoubtedly the result of events such as Ayotzinapa as turning points or "Enough is enough" moments in Mexican history.

CONCLUSION

1. To protect her identity, Belén's actual name was not released.

2. Forty organizations from a broad political spectrum were part of the con-

sortium Mesa para la Libertad de Belén, including the activist group Católicas por el Derecho a Decidir (Catholics for the Right to Decide).

3. La Campaña is a federal alliance launched by feminist and women's movement groups with the support of human rights organizations, peasant collectives, student groups, and unemployed workers' associations. La Campaña claims that abortion is a public health issue and a right owed to those who can bear children (*personas gestantes*) since the return to democracy because the criminalization of abortion reflects a citizenship paradigm that discriminates against women based on gender. See http://www.abortolegal.com.ar/

4. ESI, the program for comprehensive sex education, was established by a 2006 law (Ley 26.150) to guarantee students, in both public and private schools, access to information about sexual and reproductive health. The program seeks to promote gender equality and respect for sexual diversity. The feminist collective Ni Una Menos and other social organizations have denounced drastic budget cuts affecting this program, which they claim is crucial to end the spike in cases of gender-based violence affecting the country that is rooted in patriarchal culture.

5. For discussions about the concept of "the people" and the idea of multiplicity, see María Moreno, "Interview with Horacio González," *Journal of Latin American Cultural Studies* 11.2 (2002): 151–156. On the idea of a "feminist people," see Graciela Di Marco, "Social Movement Demands in Argentina and the Constitution of a 'Feminist People,'" in *Beyond Civil Society: Activism, Participation and Protest in Latin America*, edited by Sonia Alvarez et al. (Durham, NC: Duke University Press, 2017), 122–140.

6. The name "Mothers of Plaza de Mayo" designates the group of mothers of young men and women who were abducted by the military during the 1976–1983 dictatorship. After the disappearance of their children, the women who searched for them with no luck in police departments and other official institutions started getting together and demonstrating in Plaza de Mayo across from Casa Rosada, the governmental palace. Because public gatherings of more than three people were forbidden, the mothers moved in pairs in what became known as "las rondas de las madres" (the rounds of the mothers). These rounds, the Mothers' characteristic white headscarves, and the black-and-white pictures of their missing loved ones that they carry on their chest made them world-renowned, together with their exposé of human rights violations and state terrorism.

7. Based on the iconic white headscarf worn by the Mothers of Plaza de Mayo since 1977 in their quest for "Memory, Truth, and Justice" for their disappeared children, the green scarf creates a connection between past and present human rights abuses. This is why images of eighty-eight-year-old activist Nora Cortiñas, from Madres de Plaza de Mayo Línea Fundadora, proudly displaying the green scarf and declaring herself a feminist became one of the emotional turning points within a growing "feminist tide." The image is significant because the Mothers' activism centered on motherhood as a political identity. Overlaying the white and green scarves, Cortiñas illuminates the fact that a motherhood-based activism is not antithetical to those that decouple women's bodies from motherhood as bodily destiny and social obligation.

8. See Opheli Garcia Lawler, "Women around the World Protest in Solidarity with Argentina Ahead of Historic Abortion Vote," *The Cut*, August 8, 2018, https://www.thecut.com/2018/08/argentina-world-protests-aborto-legal-ya.html; and Lauren Holter, "These #AbortoLegalYa Tweets Stand with Argentina's Push to Legalize Abortion," *Bustle*, August 8, 2018, https://www.bustle.com/p/these-abortolegalya-tweets-stand-with-argentinas-push-to-legalize-abortion-10037356

9. After passing in the lower house of Congress, the abortion bill was rejected in the senate. Both supporters and detractors of abortion rights followed on YouTube and Facebook the four-month process of deliberation, which included live-stream transmissions of speeches by celebrities and experts from both camps in Congress ahead of the vote.

10. *Personas gestantes* or *personas con capacidad de gestar* is queer and trans activists' linguistic intervention within the reproductive rights movement to extend abortion rights to trans men and gender-nonconforming people who do not identify as women.

11. See José Van Dijck, *The Culture of Connectivity: A Critical History of Social Media* (Oxford: Oxford University Press, 2013).

12. See Cecilia Palmeiro, "The Latin American Green Tide: Desire and Feminist Transversality," *Journal of Latin American Cultural Studies*, August 6, 2018, https://medium.com/@j_lacs/the-latin-american-green-tide-desire-and-feminist-transversality-56e4b85856b2

13. In their manifesto "Latin America Will Be Entirely Feminist: We Want Ourselves Alive!" Ni Una Menos uses the image of the collective scream and Visconti's film *La Terra Trema* (The earth trembles) as metaphors to convey the force of collective action: "The earth trembles because of our scream but also because of our capacity to weave nets." Unpublished English translation by Ni Una Menos. For the Spanish version, see *Página 12*, October 8, 2016, https://www.pagina12.com.ar/diario/contratapa/13-311286-2016-10-08.html

14. Hito Steyerl, "The Articulation of Protest," in *The Wretched of the Screen* (Berlin: Sternberg Press, 2012), 77-91.

15. Jodi Dean, *Democracy and Other Neoliberal Fantasies: Communicative Capitalism and Left Politics* (Durham, NC: Duke University Press, 2009), 22.

16. Dean claims that political leaders do not feel nor are pressured to respond to protesters' demands. The election of Donald Trump prompted a discussion about the efficacy of street protests and social mobilization. See Tina Rosenberg's op-ed, "The Art of Protest," *New York Times*, November 21, 2016; Nathan Heller, "Is There Any Point to Protesting?," *New Yorker*, August 21, 2017; and Michael McBride et al., "Waiting for a Perfect Protest?," *New York Times*, September 1, 2017.

17. Dean, *Democracy and Other Neoliberal Fantasies*, 22.

18. Judith Butler, *Notes toward a Performative Theory of Assembly* (Cambridge, MA: Harvard University Press, 2015).

19. On performances as bodily acts of transfer, see Diana Taylor, *The Archive and the Repertoire: Performing Cultural Memory in the Americas* (Durham, NC: Duke University Press, 2003).

20. See Wendy Hui Kyong Chun, "The Enduring Ephemeral, or the Future Is

a Memory," *Critical Inquiry* 35.1 (2008): 148–171; and Diana Taylor, "Save as . . . Knowledge and Transmission in the Age of Digital Technologies," *Imagining America*, 2010, Paper 7, http://surface.syr.edu/ia/7.

21. On social media as echo chamber, see Ricardo de Querol, interview with Zygmunt Bauman, "Social Media Are a Trap," *El País*, January 25, 2016, https://elpais.com/elpais/2016/01/19/inenglish/1453208692_424660.html

22. See Leo G. Stewart, Ahmer Arif, and Kate Starbird, "Examining Trolls and Polarization with a Retweet Network," https://faculty.washington.edu/kstarbi/examining-trolls-polarization.pdf; and Rachel Kraus, "Activists Respond to Russia's Fake Facebook Ads," *Mashable*, May 15, 2018, https://mashable.com/2018/05/15/activists-respond-russia-facebook-ads/#J8OcvGVBjgqS

Bibliography

Agamben, Giorgio. *Means without End: Notes on Politics*. Translated by Vincenzo Binetti and Cesare Casarino. Minneapolis: University of Minnesota Press, 2000.

Ahmed, Sara. "Affective Economies." *Social Text* 22.2 (2004): 117–139.

Alvarez, Sonia, et al., eds. *Beyond Civil Society: Activism, Participation and Protest in Latin America*. Durham, NC: Duke University Press, 2017.

Arditi, Benjamín. "Insurgencies Don't Have a Plan—They *Are* the Plan: Political Performatives and Vanishing Mediators." In *The Promise and Perils of Populism: Global Perspectives*, edited by Carlos de la Torre, 113–139. Lexington: University Press of Kentucky, 2014.

Arendt, Hannah. *The Human Condition*. Chicago: University of Chicago Press, 1958.

Arendt, Hannah. "Labor, Work, Action." In *The Phenomenology Reader*, edited by Dermot Moran and Timothy Mooney, 362–374. London: Routledge, 2002.

Arteaga, Roberto, and Francisco Muciño. "La historia no contada de Ayotzinapa y las Normales Rurales." *Forbes Mexico,*. December 25, 2014. http://www.forbes.com.mx/la-historia-no-contada-de-ayotzinapa-y-las-normales-rurales/

Auslander, Philip. "Digital Liveness: A Historico-Philosophical Perspective." *PAJ: A Journal of Performance and Art* 34.3 (2012): 3–11.

Auslander, Philip. *Liveness: Performance in a Mediatized Culture*. London: Routledge, 1999.

Auyero, Javier. *La protesta: Relatos de la beligerancia popular en la Argentina democrática*. Buenos Aires: Libros del Rojas, 2002.

Badiou, Alain. *Theoretical Writings*. Edited and translated by Ray Brassier and Alberto Toscano. London: Continuum, 2004.

Balsamo, Anne. "The Virtual Body in Cyberspace." In *The Cybercultures Reader*, edited by David Bell and Barbara M. Kennedy, 489–503. London: Routledge, 2000.

Basualdo, Eduardo. *Sistema político y modelo de acumulación en la Argentina: Notas sobre el transformismo argentino durante la valorización finaciera (1976–2001)*. Buenos Aires: Universidad Nacional de Quilmes Ediciones, 2001.

Bauman, Zygmunt. *Liquid Modernity*. Cambridge: Polity Press, 2000.

Bauman, Zygmunt. "Social Media Are a Trap." Interview by Ricardo de Querol. *El País*, January 25, 2016. https://elpais.com/elpais/2016/01/19/inenglish/1453208692_424660.html

Bay-Cheng, Sarah, et al. *Mapping Intermediality in Performance*. Amsterdam: Amsterdam University Press, 2010.

Bay-Cheng, Sarah. "Digital Culture." In *Performance Studies. Key Words, Concepts and Theories*, edited by Bryan Reynolds, 39–49. London: Palgrave McMillan, 2014.

Benjamin, Walter. "What Is Epic Theatre?" In *Illuminations: Essays and Reflections*, edited by Hannah Arendt, 147–154. New York: Schocken Books, 1969.

Berardi, Franco "Bifo." "Cognitarian Subjectivation." *e-flux* 20 (2010). http://www.e-flux.com/journal/cognitarian-subjectivation/.

Berlant, Lauren. *Cruel Optimism*. Durham, NC: Duke University Press, 2011.

Bishop, Claire. *Artificial Hells: Participatory Art and the Politics of Spectatorship*. New York: Verso Books, 2012.

Boal, Augusto. *Theater of the Oppressed*. Translated by Charles A. and Maria-Odilia Leal McBride. London: Pluto Press, 1979.

Bonilla, Yarimar, and Jonathan Rosa. "#Ferguson: Digital Protest, Hashtag Ethnography, and the Racial Politics of Social Media in the United States." *American Anthropologist* 119.1 (March 2017): 154–156.

Boyd, Andrew, and Dave Oswald Mitchell, eds. *Beautiful Trouble: A Toolbox for Revolution*. New York: OR Books, 2012.

boyd, danah. "Participating in the Always-On Lifestyle." In *The Social Media Reader*, edited by Michael Mandiberg, 71–76. New York: NYU Press, 2012.

Briones, Claudia, and Marcela Mendoza. *Urban Middle-Class Women's Responses to Political Crisis in Buenos Aires*. Memphis: University of Memphis Center for Research on Women, 2001.

Brunet Icart, Ignasi, and Fernanda Laura Schilman. *Convivir con el capital financiero: Corralito y movimientos ahorristas (Argentina 2001–2004)*. Caracas: Editorial Fundamentos, 2005.

Burbach, Roger. *Globalization and Postmodern Politics: From Zapatistas to High-Tech Robber Barons*. London: Pluto Press, 2001.

Butler, Judith. *Notes toward a Performative Theory of Assembly*. Cambridge, MA: Harvard University Press, 2015.

Butler, Judith, Zeynep Gambetti, and Leticia Sabsay, eds. *Vulnerability in Resistance*. Durham, NC: Duke University Press, 2016.

Cabalin, Cristian. "Neoliberal Education and Student Movements in Chile: Inequalities and Malaise." *Policy Futures in Education* 10.2 (2012): 219–228.

Calderón, Fernando, coord. "Understanding Social Conflict in Latin America." United Nations Development Programme, Fundación UNIR, Bolivia, 2013.

Camnitzer, Luis. *Conceptualism in Latin American Art: Didactics of Liberation*. Austin: University of Texas Press, 2007.

Carassai, Sebastián. "The Noisy Majority: An Analysis of the Argentine Crisis of December 2001 from the Theoretical Approach of Hardt & Negri, Laclau and Žižek." *Journal of Latin American Cultural Studies* 16.1 (2007): 45–62.

Carlsen, Laura. "Armoring NAFTA: The Battleground for Mexico's Future." *NACLA Report on the Americas* 41.5 (2008): 17–22.

Carrigan, Ana. "Chiapas: The First Post-modern Revolution?" *Fletcher Forum* 19.1 (Winter– Spring 1995): 71–98.

Carrillo Nieto, Juan José. "El neoliberalismo en Chile: Entre la legalidad y la legitimidad. Entrevista a Tomás Moulián." *Perfiles Latinoamericanos* 1.35 (January 1, 2010): 145–155.

Castells, Manuel, ed. *The Network Society: A Cross-Cultural Perspective*. Northampton, MA: Edward Elgar Publishing, 2005.

Certeau, Michel de. *The Practice of Everyday Life*. Translated by Steven F. Rendall. Berkeley: University of California Press, 1984.

Chambers-Letson, Joshua Takano. *A Race So Different: Performance and Law in Asian America*. New York: New York University Press, 2013.

Chun, Wendy Hui Kyong. *Control and Freedom: Power and Paranoia in the Age of Fiber Optics*. Cambridge, MA: MIT Press, 2006.

Chun, Wendy Hui Kyong. "The Enduring Ephemeral, or the Future Is a Memory." *Critical Inquiry* 35.1 (2008): 148–171.

Chun, Wendy Hui Kyong. *Programmed Visions: Software and Memory*. Cambridge, MA: MIT Press, 2011.

Colectivo Situaciones. *19 & 20: Notes for a New Social Protagonism*. Translated by Nate Holdren and Sebastian Touza. New York: Minor Compositions, 2011.

Coleman, Gabriella. "The Ethics of Digital Direct Action." *Aljazeera*, September 2011. http://www.aljazeera.com/indepth/opinion/2011/08/2011830845 5825769.html.

Coleman, Gabriella. *Hacker, Hoaxer, Whistleblower, Spy: The Many Faces of Anonymous*. Brooklyn, NY: Verso, 2014.

Contreras Lorenzini, María José. "A Woman Artist in the Neoliberal Chilean Jungle." In *Performance, Feminism and Affect in Neoliberal Times*, edited by Elin Diamond, Denise Varney and Candice Amich, 239–251. London: Palgrave Macmillan, 2017.

Critical Art Ensemble. *Digital Resistance. Explorations in Tactical Media*. New York: Autonomedia, 2001.

Critical Art Ensemble. *Electronic Civil Disobedience*. New York: Autonomedia, 1996.

Critical Art Ensemble. *The Electronic Disturbance*. New York: Autonomedia, 1994.

Crowley, Michael. "México's New Mission." *Time*, February 24, 2014.

Csordas, Thomas J. *Embodiment and Experience: The Existential Ground of Culture and Self*. Cambridge: Cambridge University Press, 1994.

Csordas, Thomas J. "Embodiment as a Paradigm for Anthropology." *Ethos* 18.1 (1990): 5–47.

Cullen, Deborah. *Arte ≠ Vida: Actions by Artists of the Americas, 1960–2000*. New York: El Museo del Barrio, 2008.

Cummings, Peter M. M. "Student Movement in Chile: Explaining a Protest Paradox." *Panoramas: Scholarly Platform*, February 21, 2017, http://www.panoramas.pitt.edu/health-and-society/student-movement-chile-explaining-protest-paradox

Dardot, Pierre, and Christian Laval. *The New Way of the World: On Neoliberal Society*. London: Verso, 2014.

Dávila, Arlene. "Locating Neoliberalism in Time, Space, and 'Culture.'" *American Quarterly* 66.3 (2014): 549–555.

Dean, Jodi. *Democracy and Other Neoliberal Fantasies: Communicative Capitalism and Left Politics*. Durham, NC: Duke University Press, 2009.

Deleuze, Gilles. "Postscript on the Societies of Control." *October* 59 (1992): 3–7.

De Llano, Pedro, and Xosé Lois Gutiérrez, eds. *En tiempo real: El arte mientras tiene lugar.* A Coruña: Fundación Luis Seoane, 2001.

Democracia Distribuida: Miradas de la Universidad Nómada al 15M. Universidad Nómada, 2012. http://www.universidadnomada.net/IMG/pdf/Democracia_distribuida_ebook.pdf.

Diamond, Elin. "Introduction." In *Performance and Cultural Politics*, edited by Elin Diamond, 1–14. London: Routledge, 1996.

Di Marco, Graciela. "Social Movement Demands in Argentina and the Constitution of a 'Feminist People.'" In *Beyond Civil Society: Activism, Participation and Protest in Latin America*, edited by Sonia Alvarez et al., 122–140. Durham, NC: Duke University Press, 2017.

Dixon, Steve. *Digital Performance: A History of New Media in Theater, Dance, Performance Art, and Installation.* Cambridge, MA: MIT Press, 2007.

Duggan, Lisa. *The Twilight of Equality? Neoliberalism, Cultural Politics, and the Attack on Democracy.* Boston: Beacon Press, 2003.

Durán Prieto, Jimena, and Esteban Javier Rico. "Producciones digitales anónimas." In *Piquete de ojo: Visualidades de la crisis. Argentina 2001–2003*, edited by María Ledesma and Paula Siganevich, 83–104. Buenos Aires: Ediciones FADU, 2008.

Etheridge Woodson, Stephani, and Tamara Underiner, eds. *Theatre, Performance and Change.* Cham, Switzerland: Palgrave Macmillan, 2018.

Fajardo-Hill, Cecilia, and Andrea Giunta. *Radical Women: Latin American Art, 1960–1985.* Los Angeles: Hammer Museum, University of California; New York: Del Monico Books / Prestel.

Farman, Jason. *Mobile Interface Theory: Embodied Space and Locative Media.* London: Routledge, 2012.

Fornazzari, Alessandro. *Speculative Fictions: Chilean Culture, Economics, and the Neoliberal Transition.* Pittsburgh: University of Pittsburgh Press, 2013.

Foster, Susan Leigh. "Choreographies of Protest." *Theatre Journal* 55.3 (2003): 395–412.

Freelon, Deen, Charlton D. Mcilwain, and Meredith D. Clark, "Beyond the Hashtags: #Ferguson, #BlackLivesMatter, and the Online Struggle for Offline Justice." Research report, Center for Media & Social Impact, 2016.

Friesen, Norm. "Wandering Star: The Image of the Constellation in Benjamin, Giedion, and McLuhan." July 2013. http://www.academia.edu/4032277/Wandering_Star_The_Image_of_the_Constellation_in_Benjamin_Giedion_and_McLuhan

Fuentes, Marcela A. "#NiUnaMenos (NotOneWomanLess): Hashtag Performativity, Memory, and Direct Action against Gender Violence in Argentina." In *Women Mobilizing Memory*, edited by Ayse Gul Altinay, Maria José Contreras, Zeynep Gambetti, and Alisa Solomon, 172–191. New York: Columbia University Press, 2019.

Fusco, Coco. "On-Line Simulations / Real-Life Politics: A Discussion with Ricardo Domínguez on Staging Virtual Theatre." *TDR: The Drama Review* 47.2 (2003): 151–162.

Fusco, Coco, ed. *Corpus Delecti: Performance Art of the Americas*. New York: Routledge, 2000.

Gago, Verónica. *Neoliberalism from Below: Popular Pragmatics and Baroque Economies*. Translated by Liz Mason-Desee. Durham, NC: Duke University Press, 2017.

Gallagher, Erin. *México: Articles about Bots and Trolls*. January 1, 2017. https://medium.com/@erin_gallagher/news-articles-about-bots-trolls-in-mexican-networks-7b1e551ef4a6

Galloway, Alexander R., and Eugene Thacker. *The Exploit: A Theory of Networks*. Minneapolis: University of Minnesota Press, 2007.

Gerbaudo, Paolo. *Tweets and the Streets: Social Media and Contemporary Activism*. London: Pluto; New York: distributed in the United States by Palgrave Macmillan, 2012.

Giannachi, Gabriella. *The Politics of New Media Theatre: Life*. London: Routledge, 2006.

Gilbreth, Chris, and Gerardo Otero. "Democratization in Mexico: The Zapatista Uprising and Civil Society." *Latin American Perspectives* 28.4 (July 2001): 7–29.

Giunta, Andrea. *Poscrisis: Arte argentino después de 2001*. Buenos Aires: Siglo Veintiuno Editores, 2009.

Goldberg, RoseLee. *Performance Art: From Futurism to the Present*. Rev. ed. New York: Thames & Hudson, 2001.

Gompf, Andrea. "Was the #YaMeCansé Hashtag Hijacked by EPN Twitter Bots?" *Remezcla*. December 5, 2014. http://remezcla.com/culture/was-yame-canse-hashtag-hijacked-by-epn-bots/

Graham-Jones, Jean. "Rethinking Buenos Aires Theatre in the Wake of 2001 and Emerging Structures of Resistance and Resilience." *Theatre Journal* 66.1 (2014): 37–54.

Gregg, Melissa, and Gregory J. Seigworth, eds. *The Affect Theory Reader*. Durham, NC: Duke University Press, 2010.

Guerra, Octavio. "The Open Veins of Mexico. Three Years after Ayotzinapa." In *Until We Find You: The Disappeared of Ayotzinapa*. New York: Hemi-Press, 2017. http://untilwefindyou.tome.press/chapter/the-open-veins-of-mexico/.

Hamera, Judith. "The Labors of Michael Jackson: Virtuosity, Deindustrialization, and Dancing Work." *PMLA* 127.4 (2012): 751–765.

Hammond, John. "The World Social Forum and the Emergence of Global Grassroots Politics." *New Politics* 11.2, whole number 42 (Winter 2007), https://newpol.org/issue_post/world-social-forum-and-emergence-global-grassroots-politics/

Hansen, Mark B. N. *Bodies in Code: Interfaces with New Media*. London: Routledge, 2006.

Hardt, Michael, and Antonio Negri. *Empire*. Cambridge, MA: Harvard University Press, 2000.

Harney, Stefano, and Fred Moten. *The Undercommons: Fugitive Planning and Black Study*. New York: Minor Compositions, 2013.

Harvey, David. *A Brief History of Neoliberalism*. Oxford: Oxford University Press, 2005.

Harvie, Jen. *Fair Play: Art, Performance and Neoliberalism*. New York: Palgrave Macmillan, 2013.

Hayden, Tom, ed. *The Zapatista Reader*. New York: Thunder's Mouth Press / Nation Books, 2002.

Hayles, N. Katherine. *How We Became Posthuman: Virtual Bodies in Cybernetics, Literature, and Informatics*. Chicago: University of Chicago Press, 1999.

Heathfield, Adrian, ed. *Live: Art and Performance*. London: Tate, 2004.

Hunter, Lynette. "Constellation: Engaging with Radical Devised Dance Theatre: Keith Henessy's *Sol Niger*." In *Performance, Politics, and Activism*, edited by John Rouse and Peter Lichtenfels, 132–153. Hampshire: Palgrave Macmillan, 2013.

Jackson, Giorgio, and Camila Vallejo. "Gato por liebre." *The Clinic Online*, July 14, 2011. http://www.theclinic.cl/2011/07/14/gato-por-liebre/

Jackson, Shannon. *Social Works: Performing Art, Supporting Publics*. New York: Routledge, 2011.

Jelin, Elizabeth, ed. *Women and Social Change in Latin America*. London: Zed Books, 1990.

Jenkins, Henry. *Spreadable Media: Creating Value and Meaning in a Networked Culture*. Cambridge, MA: MIT Press, 2013.

Johnson, E. Patrick. *Appropriating Blackness: Performance and the Politics of Authenticity*. Durham, NC: Duke University Press, 2003.

Jones, Amelia. *Body Art / Performing the Subject*. Minneapolis: University of Minnesota Press, 1998.

Kauffman, L. A. *Direct Action: Protest and the Reinvention of American Radicalism*. London: Verso Books, 2017.

Kember, Sarah, and Joanna Zylinska. *Life after New Media: Mediation as a Vital Process*. Cambridge, MA: MIT Press, 2014.

Kershaw, Baz. *The Radical in Performance: Between Brecht and Baudrillard*. London: Routledge, 1999.

Klein, Naomi. *The Shock Doctrine: The Rise of Disaster Capitalism*. New York: Picador, 2007.

Klein, Naomi. "The Unknown Icon." In *The Zapatista Reader*, edited by Tom Hayden, 114–122. New York: Thunder's Mouth Press / Nation Books, 2002.

Kidd, Dorothy. "Indymedia.org: A New Communications Commons." In *Cyberactivism: Online Activism in Theory and in Practice*, edited by Martha McCaughey and Michael D. Ayers, 47–69. New York: Routledge, 2003.

Kluitenberg, Eric. *Legacies of Tactical Media: The Tactics of Occupation. From Tompkins Square to Tahrir*. Amsterdam: Institute of Network Cultures, 2011.

Laird, Sam. "This Is Thriller: What Chilean Students Can Teach the Occupy Movement." *Mashable*, November 28, 2011. http://mashable.com/2011/11/28/thriller-social-media-protest-ows/#v7f5qlv_wGq9

Lane, Jill. "Digital Zapatistas." *TDR: The Drama Review* 47.2 (2003): 129–144.

Lane, Jill. "Interview with Ricardo Dominguez." Video. Hemispheric Institute of Performance and Politics, Encuentro, Monterrey, Mexico, 2001.

"Las siete modernizaciones." *Memoria Chilena* Biblioteca Nacional de Chile. http://www.memoriachilena.cl/602/w3-article-93006.html.

Lazzarato, Maurizio. "The Machine." Translated by Mary O'Neill. European Institute for Progressive Cultural Politics. 2006. http://eipcp.net/transversal/1106/lazzarato/en.

Lazzarato, Maurizio. *The Making of the Indebted Man: An Essay on the Neoliberal Condition*. Translated by Joshua David Jordan. Los Angeles: Semiotext(e), 2012.

Lepecki, André. *Singularities: Dance in the Age of Performance*. New York: Routledge, 2016.

Levy Yeyati, Eduardo, and Diego Valenzuela. *La resurrección: Historia de la poscrisis Argentina*. Buenos Aires: Editorial Sudamericana, 2007.

Lewkowicz, Ignacio. *Sucesos Argentinos: Cacerolazo y subjetividad postestatal*. Buenos Aires: Paidós, 2003.

Lionnet, Françoise, and Shu-mei Shih, eds. *Minor Transnationalism*. Durham, NC: Duke University Press, 2005.

Longoni, Ana, and Mariano Mestman. *Del Di Tella a "Tucumán Arde": Vanguardia artística y política en el '68 argentino*. Buenos Aires: Ediciones El Cielo por Asalto, 2000.

Madison, D. Soyini. *Acts of Activism: Human Rights as Radical Performance*. Cambridge, MA: Cambridge University Press, 2010.

Malini, Fábio, and Henrique Antoun. *@Internet e #rua: Ciberativismo e mobilização nas redes sociais*. Porto Alegre: Sulina, 2013.

Marazzi, Christian. *Capital and Language: From the New Economy to the War Economy*. Translated by Gregory Conti. Los Angeles: Semiotext(e), 2008.

Martin, Randy. "After Economy? Social Logics of the Derivative." *Social Text* 144 31.1 (2013): 83–106.

Marx, Karl. *Capital: A Critique of Political Economy*. Vol. 3. Translated by Ernest Untermann. Chicago: Charles H. Kerr, 1919.

Massumi, Brian. *Parables for the Virtual: Movement, Affect, Sensation*. Durham, NC: Duke University Press, 2002.

McKenzie, Jon. "Hacktivism and Machinic Performance." *Performance Paradigm* 1 (2005): 22–30.

McKenzie, Jon. *Perform, or Else: From Discipline to Performance*. London: Routledge, 2001

McKenzie, Jon, and Rebecca Schneider. "Critical Art Ensemble: Tactical Media Practitioners." *TDR: The Drama Review* 44.4 (2000): 136–150.

McPherson, Tara. "Digital." In *Keywords for American Cultural Studies*, 2nd ed., edited by Bruce Burgett and Glenn Hendler, 79–81. New York: New York University Press, 2014.

McPherson, Tara. "U.S. Operating Systems at Mid-century: The Intertwining of Race and UNIX." In *Race after the Internet*, edited by Lisa Nakamura and Peter A. Chow-White, 21–37. London: Routledge, 2012.

Medina, Eden. *Cybernetic Revolutionaries: Technology and Politics in Allende's Chile*. Cambridge, MA: MIT Press, 2011.

Minsburg, Naúm, ed. *Los guardianes del dinero: Las políticas del FMI en Argentina*. Buenos Aires: Grupo Editorial Norma, 2003.

Moreno, María. "Interview with Horacio González." *Journal of Latin American Cultural Studies* 11.2 (2002): 151–156.

Moten, Fred. *In the Break: The Aesthetics of the Black Radical Tradition*. Minneapolis: University of Minnesota Press, 2003.

Mouffe, Chantal. "Artistic Activism and Agonistic Spaces." *Art & Research* 1.2 (Summer 2007): 1–5.

Muñoz, José Esteban. *Cruising Utopia: The Then and There of Queer Futurity*. New York: New York University Press, 2009.

Muñoz, José Esteban. "Ephemera as Evidence: Introductory Notes to Queer Acts." *Women and Performance* 8, no. 2 (1996): 5–17.

Munster, Anna. *An Aesthesia of Networks: Conjunctive Experience in Art and Technology*. Cambridge, MA: MIT Press, 2013.

Munster, Anna. *Materializing New Media: Embodiment in Information Aesthetics*. Hanover: Dartmouth College Press, 2006.

Nail, Thomas. "Zapatismo and the Global Origins of Occupy." *Journal for Cultural and Religious Theory* 12.3 (2013): 20–35.

Negri, Antonio et al. *Diálogo sobre la globalización: La multitud y la experiencia argentina*. Buenos Aires: Paidós, 2003.

Palmeiro, Cecilia. "The Latin American Green Tide: Desire and Feminist Transversality." *Journal of Latin American Cultural Studies*, August 6, 2018. https://medium.com/@j_lacs/the-latin-american-green-tide-desire-and-feminist-transversality-56e4b85856b2

Papacharissi, Zizi. *Affective Publics: Sentiment, Technology, and Politics*. Oxford: Oxford University Press, 2014.

Phelan, Peggy. *Unmarked. The Politics of Performance*. London: Routledge, 1993.

Pickard, Victor. "Assessing the Radical Democracy of Indymedia: Discursive, Technical, and Institutional Constructions." *Critical Studies in Media Communication* 23.1 (2006): 19–38.

Quijano, Aníbal. "Coloniality of Power, Eurocentrism, and Latin America." *Nepantla: Views from South* 1.3 (2000): 533–581.

Raley, Rita. *Tactical Media*. Minneapolis: University of Minnesota Press, 2009.

Ramos, Laura, ed. *El fracaso del Consenso de Washington. La caída de su mejor alumno: Argentina*. Barcelona: Icaria Editorial, 2003.

Rancière, Jacques. *The Politics of Aesthetics: The Distribution of the Sensible*. Translated by Gabriel Rockhill. London: Continuum, 2006.

Ranis, Peter. "Factories without Bosses: Argentina's Experience with Worker-Run Enterprises." *Labor: Studies in Working-Class History of the Americas* 3.1 (2006): 11–24.

Reed, T. V. *The Art of Protest: Culture and Activism from the Civil Rights Movement to the Streets of Seattle*. Minneapolis: University of Minnesota Press, 2005.

Reguillo, Rossana. *Paisajes insurrectos: Jóvenes, redes y revueltas en el otoño civilizatorio*. NED Ediciones, 2017. Kindle.

Reguillo, Rosana. "The Narco-Machine and the Work of Violence: Notes toward Its Identification." *e-misférica* 8.2. http://hemisphericinstitute.org/hemi/en/e-misferica-82/reguillo.

Reguillo, Rossana. "Rostros en escenas: La imposibilidad del desentendimiento." *Magis*, ITESO. (ITESO), December 1, 2014, https://magis.iteso.mx/content/rostros-en-escenas-ayotzinapa-y-la-imposibilidad-del-desentendimiento

Rheingold, Howard. *Smart Mobs: The Next Social Revolution*. Cambridge: Basic Books, 2002.

Richard, Nelly. *Margins and Institutions: Art in Chile since 1973*. Melbourne: Art and Text, 1986.

Roach, Joseph. *Cities of the Dead: Circum-Atlantic Performance*. New York: Columbia University Press, 1996.

Roman, Richard, and Edur Velasco Arregui. "The Specter of Ayotzinapa Haunts the Continent." *NACLA Reporting on the Americas*, December 8, 2014. https://nacla.org/news/2014/12/07/spectre-ayotzinapa-haunts-continent

Salter, Chris. *Entangled: Technology and the Transformation of Performance*. Cambridge, MA: MIT Press, 2010.

Sánchez Cedillo, Raúl. "El 15 M como insurrección del cuerpo máquina." In *Democracia Distribuida: Miradas de la Universidad Nómada al 15M*, 49–65. Universidad Nómada, 2012.

Schatzman, Christina. "Political Challenge in Latin America: Rebellion and Collective Protest in an Era of Democratization." *Journal of Peace Research* 42.3 (2005): 291–310.

Schechner, Richard. *Between Theater and Anthropology*. Philadelphia: University of Pennsylvania Press, 1985.

Scheible, Jeff. *Digital Shift: The Cultural Logic of Punctuation*. Minneapolis: University of Minnesota Press, 2015.

Schiller, Daniel. *Digital Capitalism: Networking the Global Market System*. Cambridge, MA: MIT Press, 1999.

Schimmel, Paul. "Leap into the Void: Performance and the Object." In *Out of Actions: Between Performance and the Object, 1949–1979*, edited by Russell Ferguson, 17–120. London: Thames and Hudson, 1998.

Schneider, Rebecca. "It Seems as If . . . I Am Dead: Zombie Capitalism and Theatrical Labor." *TDR: The Drama Review* 56.4 (2012): 150–162.

Schneider, Rebecca. "Performance Remains." *Performing Research* 6.2 (2001): 100–108.

Sharma, Sanjay. "Black Twitter? Racial Hashtags, Networks and Contagion." *New Formations* 78 (Summer 2012): 46–64.

Sitrin, Marina. "One No, Many Yeses," in *Occupy! Scenes from Occupied America*, edited by Astra Taylor et al., 7–11. London: Verso, 2011.

Sitrin, Marina. "Pulling the Emergency Break." *Tidal: Occupy Theory, Occupy Strategy* 2 (2012): 6–7.

Smith, Adam. *The Wealth of Nations: Books I–IV*. Edited by Andrew Skinner. London: Penguin Books, 1999.

Smucker, Jonathan Matthew. *Hegemony How-to: A Roadmap for Radicals*. Baltimore: AK Press, 2017.

Steyerl, Hito. *The Wretched of the Screen*. Berlin: Sternberg Press, 2012.

Subcomandante Insurgente Galeano. "Between Light and Shadow." *Enlace Zapatista*. http://enlacezapatista.ezln.org.mx/2014/05/27/between-light-and-shadow/.

Subcomandante Marcos. "First Declaration from the Lacandón Jungle." In *The Zapatista Reader*, edited by Tom Hayden, 217–220. New York: Thunder's Mouth Press / Nation Books, 2002.

Subcomandante Marcos. "Fourth Declaration from the Lacandón Jungle." In *The Zapatista Reader*, edited by Tom Hayden, 239–249. New York: Thunder's Mouth Press / Nation Books, 2002.

Tabachnik, Silvia. "La construcción del acontecimiento en la era de Internet." *Mediaciones de la Comunicación* 11 (2016): 181–195.

Tambakaki, Paulina. "The Tasks of Agonism and Agonism to the Task: Introducing 'Chantal Mouffe: Agonism and the Politics of Passion.' " *parallax* 20.2 (2014): 1–13.

Taylor, Astra, et al., eds. *Occupy!: Scenes from Occupied America*. London: Verso, 2011.

Taylor, Diana. *The Archive and the Repertoire: Performing Cultural Memory in the Americas*. Durham, NC: Duke University Press, 2003.

Taylor, Diana. "Dancing with the Zapatistas." In *Dancing with the Zapatistas Twenty Year Later*, edited by Diana Taylor and Lorie Novak. Durham, NC: Duke University Press; New York: HemiPress, 2015. http://scalar.usc.edu/ anvc/dancing-with-the-zapatistas/zapatistas

Taylor, Diana. "Interview with Diamela Eltit." In *What Is Performance Studies?*, edited by Diana Taylor and Marcos Steuernagel. Durham, NC: Duke University Press; New York: HemiPress, 2015. http://scalar.usc.edu/nehvectors/ wips/diamela-eltit-english

Taylor, Diana. "Save as . . . Knowledge and Transmission in the Age of Digital Technologies." *Imagining America*, 2010. Paper 7. http://surface.syr.edu/ia/7.

Terranova, Tiziana. *Network Culture: Politics for the Information Age*. London: Pluto Press, 2004.

Toret, Javier, et al. "Tecnopolítica: La potencia de las multitudes conectadas. El sistema red 15M, un nuevo paradigma de la política distribuida." Internet Disciplinary Institute, IN3 Working Paper Series RR-13-001, June 18, 2013. http://tecnopolitica.net/sites/default/files/1878-5799-3-PB%20(2).pdf

Treré, Emiliano. "The Dark Side of Digital Politics: Understanding the Algorithmic Manufacturing of Consent and the Hindering of Online Dissidence." *IDS Bulletin* 47.1 (January 24, 2016), http://bulletin.ids.ac.uk/idsbo/ article/view/41.

Truffin, Sherry R. "Zombies in the Classroom: Education as Consumption in Two Novels by Joyce Carol Oates." In *Zombies in the Academy: Living Death in Higher Education*, edited by Andrew Whelan, Ruth Walker, and Christopher Moore, 203–215. Chicago: University of Chicago Press, 2013.

Urra Rossi, Juan. "La movilización estudiantil chilena en 2011: Una cronología." *OSAL: Observatorio Social de América Latina* 13.31 (2012): 23–38.

Valenzuela, Sebastián, et al. "The Social Media Basis of Youth Protest Behavior: The Case of Chile." *Journal of Communication* 62.2 (2012): 299–314.

Van Dijck, José. *The Culture of Connectivity: A Critical History of Social Media*. Oxford: Oxford University Press, 2013.

Virilio, Paul. *Speed and Politics: An Essay on Dromology*. Translated by Mark Polizzotti. Los Angeles: Semiotext(e), 2006.

Waters, Malcolm. *Globalization*. 2nd ed. London: Routledge, 2001.

Watkins Fisher, Anna. "Introduction to Network-Events." In *New Media, Old Media: A History and Theory Reader*, edited by Wendy Hui Kyong Chun,

Anna Watkins Fisher, and Thomas Keenan, 302–306. New York: Routledge, 2015.

Weltevrede, Esther, Anne Helmond, and Carolin Gerlitz. "The Politics of Real-Time: A Device Perspective on Social Media Platforms and Search Engines." *Theory, Culture & Society* 31.6 (2014): 125–150.

Werth, Brenda. *Theatre, Performance, and Memory Politics in Argentina*. New York: Palgrave Macmillan, 2010.

Wickstrom, Maurya. *Performance in the Blockades of Neoliberalism: Thinking the Political Anew*. Basingstoke: Palgrave Macmillan, 2012.

Wright, Peter, and John McCarthy. *Technology as Experience*. Cambridge, MA: MIT Press, 2004.

Ybarra, Patricia. *Latinx Theater in the Times of Neoliberalism*. Evanston, IL: Northwestern University Press, 2018.

Zappavigna, Michele, "Ambient Affiliation: A Linguistic Perspective on Twitter." *New Media & Society* 13.5 (2011): 788–806.

Zenobi, Diego. Protesta social, violencia y performances: Narraciones de *orden* y prácticas de *desorden* en las marchas de los 'ahorristas estafados.' Master's thesis, Universidad de Buenos Aires, 2004.

Index

Abramović, Marina, 14, 15

Acteal massacre, 31, 35–37

action art, 13

acts of transfer, 16, 62, 76; of memory transfer, 113

aesthetics, performative function of, 71; as self-styling, 73

affect: defined, 126n50, 136n32; networked, 19; symbolic action as affective connector, 36; affective force, 68 (*see also* eventness); affective capitalism, 77; affective publics, 84; hashtags and, 89–91; Twitter's affective economy, 90

affiliation, 89, 90, 91, 144n6

Agamben, Giorgio, 127n65

agit-prop theater, 24

agonism, 113, 123n10; "agonistic scenes," 26

Alcaraz, María Florencia, 64

algorithms: algorithmic choreography, 104; activist performance as algorithm, 104; Twitter algorithms, 90, 93, 110, 142n36; algorithm performance, 117n17

Allende, Salvador, 9, 81

Anonymous (hacktivist group), 25–26, 57

Anonymous Digital Coalition, 31

antiglobalization movement, 18, 24, 27–28, 31, 43–44, 45, 52–54, 112

appearance, space of, 11, 120n38

Arab Spring, 19

Arditi, Benjamin, 118n13

Arendt, Hannah, 11

Argentina: bank customers' protests in, 58–63; digital tactics in, 52–58;

dissidents disappeared from, 17, 49, 107; economic crisis protests in, 2, 3, 7, 18, 21, 43–48, 50–65, 93; gender violence protests in, 10–11; grassroots projects in, 50–51; neoliberalism in, v, 9, 10, 48–50, 52; reproductive rights movement in, 2, 21–22, 64, 107–11; Unemployed Workers Movement in, 17, 111; *Argentinazo*, 135n20. *See also* pots-and-pans protests

Argentina2001.ppt campaign, 43, 44, 54–55, 57

Auslander, Philip, 14, 79

Ayotzinapa students disappearance, 2, 3–4, 5–6, 10–11, 21, 36, 37, 91–93, 95–98, 100–104; "Quisieron enterrarnos, pero no sabían que éramos semilla" statement, 5–6, 97, 115

Badiou, Alain, 83, 98

Bakhtin, Mikhail, 133n2

Balsamo, Anne, 125n33

Barrancos, Dora, 111

Bauman, Zygmunt, 76, 145n21

"Belén," 107, 108

Bellucci, Mabel, 51

Benjamin, Walter, 40

Berardi, Franco, 69

Bishop, Claire, 40–41

Black Lives Matter, 90, 99, 138n7, 139n8

Boal, Augusto, 40

bodies. *See* embodiment

bots, 95, 142n36; Peña bots, 140n16

boyd, danah, 14

Bonilla, Yarimar, 89–90, 99
Brecht, Bertolt, 39–40
Bretton Woods agreement, 49
"bring-in" performance constellations, 58, 61, 62
Buenos Aires Performance Biennial, 15
Burden, Chris, 14
Butler, Judith, 11, 112

Cabalin, Cristian, 69
cacerolazos. See pots-and-pans protests
CADA (Art Actions Collective), 71
Cájas, Edison, 80
Calderón, Felipe, 101
Camnitzer, Luis, 13
Campaña Nacional por el Derecho al Aborto Legal, Seguro y Gratuito, 107, 108–11, 149n3
Carassai, Sebastián, 64
Castells, Manuel, 34, 132n47
Casullo, Nicolás, 64
Cavallo, Domingo, 45, 59
Certeau, Michel de, 37–38
Chambers-Letson, Joshua, 38
Chile: "fearless generation" in, 70–71, 80; neoliberalism in, 9, 49, 68–69, 77, 82–83, 86; student protests in, 2, 3, 6, 21, 67–87
choreography and protests, 3–4, 7, 92. *See also Thriller por la educación*
Chun, Wendy Hui Kyong, 6, 79, 99–100
citizen journalism, 18, 21, 53
"clicktivism," 19
Cocco, Giuseppe, v
Colectivo Etcétera, 51
Colectivo Situaciones, 50
Coleman, Gabriella, 32
colonial legacies (and neocolonialism), 4, 10, 22, 25, 29, 42, 103; "coloniality of power," 142n40
CONFECH (Chilean Students' Confederation), 70
convergence tactics, 20, 25–26, 30, 32, 33, 42, 44, 48, 112; flash mobs

and, 79, 86; hashtags and, 89, 108
corralito financiero, 45, 50, 59
Critical Art Ensemble, 17, 39
Crowley, Michael, 93
Csordas, Thomas, 125n35

Dean, Jodi, 78, 111–12
Dawkins, Richard, 139n12
1,800 Hours for Education, 67–68, 80–85
debt issues, 21, 68–70, 78, 80, 84–87; Argentina's sovereign debt, 49; "debt governance," 70, 134n15; http//:www.YoDebo.cl, 82–83
de la Rúa, Fernando, 46
détournement, 95
Diamond, Elin, 38
digital activism, 2, 16–20; superseded by social media, 64–65
digital archives, 78–79
digital capitalism, 58, 61
digital memory, 100
digital networking, 2–4, 7, 15, 17, 19–20, 108, 111; "machinic performances" and, 35
digital storytelling, 15, 21, 55, 57
Dillon, Marta, 107–8
Di Marco, Graciela, 64
disappearance: as capital flight, 62; as hemispheric history, 37, 96; as performance ontology, 14, 118nn11–12; as repressive strategy, 17, 49, 101, 107
"distributed democracy," 19, 135n31, 142n42
distributed denial of service attacks (DDos), 24, 25, 32
Dominguez, Ricardo, 31, 32, 38–40
Dixon, Steve, 14
Duggan, Lisa, 8
Durán Prieto, Jimena, 55

Educación Sexual Integral, 107, 143n4
education, financing of, 68–70
electronic civil disobedience, 4, 17, 20, 24–25, 31, 37, 42
Electronic Disturbance Theater